JOHN WAYNE
Family Cookbook

Recipes and Recollections from Duke's Kitchen to Yours

Aissa, Pilar, Patrick and Duke on the set of *McLintock!* (1963). The movie was produced by son Michael and also starred Duke's friend Maureen O'Hara, making a work day feel more like a family reunion.

My father knew the family that shared meals together shared much more than food—they made memories, gave each other advice and strengthened the bonds of love and tradition this country was built on. That's why we've collected these delicious, authentic recipes for any occasion. Once your family catches the scent of what you're cooking in the kitchen, you'll have more trouble keeping them away from the table than getting them around it. From our family to yours, we hope you enjoy.

Dig in,

Ethan Wayne

Contents

Duke and his youngest son Ethan enjoy a moment on the set of *Rio Lobo* (1970). The movie was the last in the career of director Howard Hawks, a Hollywood legend in his own right.

Up and At 'Em

Start your day off on the right foot
with these mouth-watering breakfasts that
will keep you sated all day long.

Maple Pancakes

Sausage and Spinach Strata

Brannigan's Banana Walnut Muffins

Eggs Baked in Tomato Sauce

Spanish Tortilla

Ringo Kid's Bacon Pancakes

Classic Scratch Biscuits

Blueberry Pancakes

Davy Crockett's Breakfast Casserole

MAPLE PANCAKES

These pancakes will have your family flipping out over flapjacks in a whole new way.

MAKES 13 PANCAKES

SUPPLIES

12 slices thick-cut bacon

¾ cup plus 2 Tbsp. oats

¾ cup flour

½ cup cornstarch

1½ tsp. baking powder

½ tsp. baking soda

½ tsp. kosher salt

1 cup buttermilk

2 large eggs

¼ cup maple syrup

2 Tbsp. bacon grease

DIRECTIONS

Preheat oven to 200 degrees F.

Cut the bacon in half lengthwise, and then cut into ½-inch pieces. Put in a large, cold skillet and turn the heat to medium. Cook the bacon, stirring frequently, until browned and crispy, about 10 minutes. Remove the bacon pieces from the grease with a slotted spoon and drain on paper towels. Reserve 1 Tbsp. of bacon grease for the batter and a little for greasing the pancake griddle.

Put the oats in a blender or food processor and grind to a powder. Add the flour, cornstarch, baking powder and soda, salt, buttermilk, eggs, maple syrup and 1 Tbsp. reserved bacon grease. Blend until combined, scraping down the sides of the blender or food processor once or twice. Let batter sit for 10 minutes to thicken slightly. Reserve a small handful of the bacon pieces for garnish and fold the rest into the batter.

Heat a griddle or large skillet over medium-low. Brush with some reserved bacon grease and pour or ladle about ¼ cup of batter out for each pancake. Cook until the edges of the pancake start to look dry and there are some holes in the top of the pancakes, about 1 ½ minutes. Flip and cook until the bottoms are browned and the pancakes feel firm to the touch, about another minute. Put pancakes on a plate and keep warm in the oven while cooking remaining batter.

DID YOU KNOW?

Duke and John Ford had a personal and professional relationship that was one of the deepest bonds in either man's life. Ford was even the godfather to Duke's sons Ethan and Patrick.

SAUSAGE AND SPINACH STRATA

Sure, you can start your day off eating something besides meat and cheese. But why would you want to when you can easily whip together this dish?

SERVES 10

SUPPLIES

- 1 Tbsp. olive oil
- 1 medium onion, diced
- 1 lb. mild Italian or country sausage, crumbled
- 1 (10-oz.) box fresh or frozen spinach, thawed
- 1 tsp. kosher salt
- ½ tsp. pepper
- 8 slices bread, cut into cubes
- 2 cups shredded cheddar cheese
- 12 eggs
- 2 cups milk
- 1 tsp. dry mustard powder

DIRECTIONS

In a large skillet, heat the olive oil over medium-high. Add the onion and cook until tender, about 5 minutes. Add the sausage and cook through until no longer pink, about 5 more minutes. Drain off any fat from the pan. Squeeze the spinach dry and add to the pan with the onions and sausage, add a big pinch of salt and pepper and cook for 2 minutes. Remove from heat.

Layer the bread cubes on the bottom of a 9- by 12-inch (or similar sized) baking dish. Add the sausage and spinach mixture then top with the cheese.

In a mixing bowl, whisk the eggs with the milk, salt, pepper and mustard powder. Pour the egg mixture into the baking dish. Cover and refrigerate for about 8 hours or overnight.

Preheat oven to 350 degrees F. Remove the strata from the refrigerator and let sit at room temperature while the oven preheats. Bake the strata for 50 to 60 minutes or until everything is set. Let cool a few minutes and serve.

WAYNE FAMILY TIP

This is a great breakfast for when you need to get an early start to the day. Put it together before turning in and put it in the oven in the morning.

15

BRANNIGAN'S BANANA WALNUT MUFFINS

Whether you're a detective on the case or just running a little behind, there's not always time for a sit-down meal. These muffins all but guarantee you'll never miss a filling and delicious breakfast.

MAKES 18 MUFFINS

SUPPLIES

1½ cups all-purpose flour

1 cup sugar

1 tsp. baking powder

½ tsp. baking soda

½ tsp. kosher salt

3 ripe bananas

8 Tbsp. (1 stick) unsalted butter, melted

½ cup whole milk

1 large egg

1 tsp. pure vanilla extract

1 cup chopped walnuts

DIRECTIONS

Preheat oven to 350 degrees F. Line 18 standard sized muffin cups with paper liners.

In a medium bowl, whisk together the flour, sugar, baking powder, baking soda and salt.

In a large mixing bowl, mash 2 of the bananas well with a fork. Add the melted butter, milk, egg and vanilla, and whisk well. Add the banana mixture to the flour mixture and stir until all the flour is blended into the batter. Dice the remaining banana and fold into the batter along with the nuts. Divide the batter evenly among the prepared muffin cups.

Bake the muffins for 30 to 35 minutes, or until golden brown and a toothpick inserted into the center comes out clean. Let cool for 5 minutes in the pan.

WAYNE FAMILY TIP

Stir only until all of your dry mixture is moistened, but don't try to stir out all the lumps or your muffins will be tough.

EGGS BAKED IN TOMATO SAUCE

When you feel the breakfast standards are getting a little too familiar for your family, try this fresh take on eggs and watch your loved ones fight for seconds.

SERVES 4

SUPPLIES

- 1 Tbsp. olive oil
- 1 medium onion, diced
- 1 garlic clove, minced
- 1 (15-oz.) can of diced tomatoes
- 1½ cups tomato sauce
- Kosher salt and pepper, to taste
- 8 large eggs
- ¼ cup Parmesan cheese, grated (optional)

DIRECTIONS

Preheat oven to 350 degrees F.

In a large skillet, heat the olive oil over medium-high. Add the onion and cook for 5 minutes or until softened. Add the garlic and cook for 30 more seconds. Add the canned tomatoes along with the juice and cook for about 10 minutes or until the liquid has evaporated. Add the tomato sauce and cook for another 5 minutes. Season to taste with salt and pepper.

Divide the sauce among four 12-ounce, oven-proof ramekins, bowls or mini skillets. Crack two eggs on top of the sauce in each ramekin and sprinkle the eggs with a little salt and pepper. Sprinkle the Parmesan on top and bake for 10 minutes or until the whites are set and the yolks are still soft.

DID YOU KNOW?

Duke enjoyed hearty breakfasts, which were never without eggs. "At breakfast, he'd have a plate of eggs and a separate plate just piled with crispy bacon," Ethan Wayne remembers.

SPANISH TORTILLA

Say hola to your family's new favorite breakfast.

SERVES 6 AS A MAIN DISH, OR 8–10 AS AN APPETIZER

SUPPLIES

- 1 lb. Mexican chorizo
- 1½ lb. baby Yukon Gold potatoes, sliced ⅛-inch thick
- Kosher salt and pepper, to taste
- 1 small red onion, thinly sliced
- 12 eggs, lightly beaten
- 4 oz. soft goat cheese, crumbled or cut into small pieces

DIRECTIONS

Remove the casings from the chorizo and place in a 12-inch nonstick, oven-proof skillet. Cook over medium heat until the sausage is fully cooked and has rendered its fat. With a slotted spoon, remove the cooked sausage and drain on paper towels.

Drain all but 2 Tbsp. of the fat from the skillet, add the potatoes and a large pinch of salt and pepper. Cook over medium heat for 10 minutes, gently stirring occasionally. You want the potatoes to cook through but not brown; if they start to brown, reduce the heat. Add the onions and cook for another 5 minutes, stirring occasionally, or until the onions are soft and the potatoes are fork tender and just starting to brown.

Reduce heat to low, pour in the chorizo, the beaten eggs and goat cheese and gently pull the edges of the egg mixture to the center as it cooks so that any uncooked eggs run underneath.

Preheat the broiler. Once the eggs are set around the edges and the mixture looks mostly cooked, place the skillet under the broiler for 2 to 3 minutes or until the eggs are fully set and the tortilla is golden and slightly puffed.

Run a dinner knife around the edges of the tortilla to loosen it and slide onto a serving plate or cutting board. The tortilla can be served hot, warm, at room temperature or cold. Cut into wedges and serve.

DID YOU KNOW?

John Wayne appeared in nearly 200 films in his 50-year-long acting career. That averages out to almost four films a year. If he had time for breakfast, so should you.

RINGO KID'S BACON PANCAKES

These sweet and savory treats are so good, they should be outlawed.

MAKES ABOUT 20 PANCAKES

SUPPLIES

10 slices of bacon

4 Tbsp. bacon grease

1½ cups all-purpose flour

1½ cups cornmeal

½ tsp. kosher salt

1 Tbsp. baking powder

1½ tsp. baking soda

2 large eggs

3 Tbsp. maple syrup, plus more for serving

1 Tbsp. pure vanilla extract

2-2½ cups buttermilk

Butter, for cooking the pancakes

DIRECTIONS

Preheat the oven to 200 degrees F.

Cut the bacon in small pieces. Place in a large skillet and cook over medium heat, stirring occasionally, until very crispy, 12 to 15 minutes. Remove the bacon with a slotted spoon and drain the bacon on paper towels. Reserve 4 Tbsp. of bacon grease, more if you want to cook the pancakes in bacon grease instead of butter.

In a large mixing bowl, whisk together the flour, cornmeal, salt, baking powder and baking soda.

In a separate bowl, whisk together the eggs, 3 Tbsp. maple syrup, vanilla and 2 cups buttermilk. Add the wet ingredients to the dry ingredients and stir to combine. Stir in the reserved bacon grease. If the batter is too thick, add a little more buttermilk. Stir in half of the cooked bacon.

Heat a skillet over medium-low until hot. Melt about 1 Tbsp. of butter on the skillet and ladle ¼ cup of batter per pancake. Cook until the edges of the pancake start to look dry and the bottom is golden brown, about 3 minutes. Flip and cook another 2 to 3 minutes or until golden brown. Put on a heatproof plate and keep warm in the oven while cooking the rest of the pancakes.

Serve the pancakes with maple syrup and the rest of the bacon on top.

WAYNE FAMILY TIP

For a more decorative look, you can place the bacon pieces back in the pan and pour the ¼ cup of batter over the bacon.

From left, Patrick Wayne, director John Farrow and Duke hang out on the set of *Hondo* (1953). Out of all the Wayne siblings, Patrick appeared alongside his father on-screen the most.

CLASSIC SCRATCH BISCUITS

The recipe for these homestyle country biscuits is a lot like a family heirloom, something to treasure, then pass on.

SERVES 12

SUPPLIES

- 1½ cups flour, plus more for rolling
- ¾ cup cornstarch
- 1 Tbsp. baking powder
- 1 tsp. kosher or fine sea salt
- 6 Tbsp. butter, cut into small pieces
- ¾ cup milk

DIRECTIONS

Preheat oven to 400 degrees F. Line a baking sheet with parchment paper or a silicone baking mat.

Whisk together the flour, starch, baking powder and salt. Cut the butter into the flour either with a pastry cutter, two knives or by rubbing the butter into the flour with your fingers. Make sure you leave some larger pieces of butter. Add the liquid, starting with ½ cup and gradually adding a little more at a time, mixing until the dough comes together.

Put a little flour on a work surface and dump out the dough. Knead 3 or 4 times then either roll or pat it out to about ½-inch thick. Cut into biscuits using a 2 ½-inch cookie cutter. You can gently reform the dough to cut more biscuits.

Place the biscuits on the prepared baking sheet and bake for 20 minutes or until lightly browned. Serve warm.

WAYNE
FAMILY TIP

Make sure your butter is cold at the start to achieve maximum flakiness.

BLUEBERRY PANCAKES

This is a classic breakfast food that'll be welcome at any table.

SERVES 12

SUPPLIES

- 2 cups pancake mix
- 2 large eggs
- 1 cup milk
- 1 Tbsp. sugar
- Grapeseed or vegetable oil, for cooking
- 1½ cups fresh or frozen blueberries (defrost if frozen)

DIRECTIONS

Preheat oven to 200 degrees F.

In a large mixing bowl, whisk together the pancake mix, eggs, milk and sugar. Heat a skillet or griddle over medium until a drop of water sprinkled on the pan sizzles immediately. Brush the pan with oil and let heat for a few seconds.

Ladle a scant ¼ cup of pancake batter onto the pan for each pancake. Sprinkle about 2 Tbsp. of blueberries on top of the batter. Let cook until the bottoms are browned, the edges look dry and tiny bubbles appear on the surface of the pancake, about 5 minutes. Flip and cook for another minute or until the bottoms are browned. Keep the cooked pancakes warm in the oven while preparing the rest. Serve warm.

WAYNE FAMILY TIP

Avoid pressing down on the pancakes as you cook them. You want them light and fluffy, not dense!

DAVY CROCKETT'S BREAKFAST CASSEROLE

Start your day with this hearty meal and you'll have enough energy to defend the Alamo (or anything else).

SERVES 8–10

SUPPLIES

- 6 bacon slices, diced
- 1 cup diced green peppers
- 1 cup diced yellow onion
- 3 cups peeled and diced sweet potatoes
- 1 tsp. salt
- 1 tsp. garlic powder
- 1 tsp. onion powder
- 1 lb. breakfast sausage
- 1 (9-oz.) package fresh spinach
- 12 large eggs

DIRECTIONS

Preheat oven to 350 degrees F.

In a saucepan over medium heat, cook the bacon until it renders a good amount of fat. Add the peppers, onion, sweet potatoes, salt, garlic powder and onion powder.

Cook for 5 minutes, stirring continuously. Add the breakfast sausage. Crumble it up as it cooks for 2 to 3 minutes. Add the spinach and stir until wilted. (Covering the saucepan will speed this up.)

Transfer the mixture to a 9- by 13-inch casserole dish, spreading it evenly and pressing down.

Crack the eggs on top. Bake until the egg whites are set and yolks are done to your liking, 5 to 10 minutes for slightly runny yolks or longer for firmer yolks.

DID YOU KNOW?

John Wayne cared so much about the history of the Alamo that he decided to make his directorial debut a feature film about the battle there. 1960's *The Alamo* earned an Academy Award nomination for Best Picture.

In-Between Bites

///

For the days when three square meals just won't cut it,
these easy-to-make recipes will tide you over 'til chow time.

TERIYAKI CHICKEN WINGS

You can't go wrong with this sweet and savory snack, no matter where you are.

SERVES 8

SUPPLIES

- ½ cup teriyaki sauce
- ½ cup honey
- 3 lb. chicken wing drummettes
- 2 tsp. toasted sesame seeds

DIRECTIONS

Preheat oven to 475 degrees F. Line 2 rimmed baking sheets with foil.

Combine the teriyaki sauce with the honey. Pour half the mixture into a large mixing bowl, add the chicken wings and toss to coat. Place the chicken wings on the prepared baking sheets, skin side down and bake for 20 minutes. Discard any leftover marinade.

Remove 2 Tbsp. from the remaining teriyaki and honey mixture. Pour the remaining sauce into a small serving bowl. Turn the chicken wings over, brush with the 2 Tbsp. of sauce and cook for another 2 minutes. Sprinkle the wings with the sesame seeds and serve with the reserved sauce for dipping.

WAYNE
FAMILY TIP

Serve your wings with some lime wedges to add another layer of flavor to this snack.

SCALLOPED TOMATOES

This refreshing dish is best shared with folks who appreciate simple, good-tasting food. Or just keep them all to yourself!

SERVES 6

SUPPLIES

- 2 lb. plum tomatoes
- 1 Tbsp. fresh rosemary, minced
- 2 Tbsp. balsamic vinegar
- 2 Tbsp. olive oil
- 5 garlic cloves, minced or grated
- 2 tsp. kosher or fine sea salt
- 1 tsp. pepper
- 1½ cups panko style breadcrumbs, divided

DIRECTIONS

Preheat oven to 350 degrees F.

Cut the tomatoes into roughly 1-inch pieces. Place in an 8- by 8-inch (or similar sized) baking dish. Add the rosemary, balsamic vinegar, olive oil, minced garlic cloves, salt, pepper and 1 cup of the breadcrumbs, and toss well.

Bake for 25 minutes. Top with the remaining ½ cup of breadcrumbs and cook for 10 more minutes or until the top is nicely browned.

WAYNE
FAMILY TIP

Put some olive oil or butter on top of the breadcrumbs so they brown more evenly.

John Wayne, daughter Aissa and wife Pilar gathered around the table. When Duke was a child, he didn't always get to eat his fill, which made him all the more grateful for his later (well-earned) success.

ALL-AMERICAN ONION RINGS

The perfect snack to chow down on in the company of friends and family on a hot summer afternoon—or anytime.

SERVES 4–5

SUPPLIES

- 2 large white onions
- 2½ tsp. kosher or fine sea salt
- 2 tsp. black pepper
- 2 cups buttermilk
- 1½ cups flour
- ¼ cup yellow cornmeal
- 1 qt. vegetable oil

DIRECTIONS

Preheat oven to 200 degrees F.

Prepare a baking sheet by lining it with paper towels.

Peel onions and slice them ½ to ¾ inch thick. Separate into rings.

In a bowl, add 1 tsp. of salt and 1 tsp. of pepper to the buttermilk. Drop the onion rings into the buttermilk mixture and let set for half an hour (can sit as long as a few hours). Mix the flour and cornmeal with 1 ½ tsp. of salt and 1 tsp. of pepper.

Heat the vegetable oil in a large pot or Dutch oven to 275 degrees F. Working in small batches, take some onion rings out of the buttermilk and dredge in the flour mixture, then carefully drop into the hot oil. Make sure you do not over crowd. Fry for about 2 minutes or until golden brown turning once during frying. Take onion rings out of the oil and put on the prepared baking sheet and sprinkle with some additional salt. Keep them warm in the oven while you fry the rest of the onion rings.

Serve hot.

DID YOU KNOW?

John Wayne excelled at football while attending Glendale High School, proving himself as a star player on a championship team. He also covered the action as a sportswriter for the school's paper, the *Explosion*. He later earned a football scholarship to USC.

COWBOY SALSA

Keep the dudes and buckaroos in your life happy with this classic, spicy mix.

SERVES 8–10

SUPPLIES

- 1 package black bean soup mix
- 1 red onion, diced
- 2 tomatoes, seeded and diced
- 2 cups fresh or frozen corn kernels (thawed if frozen)
- 1 (14-oz.) can sliced pickled carrots, drained (optional)
- 1 bunch cilantro, roughly chopped
- 2 limes, juiced
- ¼ cup olive oil
- Kosher salt and pepper, to taste

DIRECTIONS

Rinse and sort beans, reserve the flavor pack. Place the beans in a large pot and cover with 2 inches of warm water. Allow the beans to soak overnight or at least 4 hours.

Drain the water from the beans and fill the pot with fresh water, at least 8 cups. Add the flavor packet, cover the pot and bring to a boil. Reduce heat to a simmer and let beans cook for 1 hour 30 minutes to 2 hours or until the beans are tender. Drain beans.

Combine the cooked beans with the remaining ingredients and refrigerate for at least 2 hours.

DID YOU KNOW?
Duke loved salsa—so much so that he'd even pour it over his bacon at breakfast.

John Wayne, son Michael (right) and a friend get ready for some traveling. Michael produced many of his father's movies, including *McLintock!* (1963) and *The Green Berets* (1968).

CHEESY BREADSTICKS

Duke loved classic Italian cuisine, and these pieces of culinary perfection are another way to enjoy the tastes of the Old Country.

SERVES 8

SUPPLIES

- 1 (7.5-oz.) box breadstick mix
- 1½ cups grated Parmesan cheese, divided
- 2 large eggs
- 2 Tbsp. olive oil, plus more for brushing the breadsticks
- ¼ cup water
- 8 oz. mozzarella or string cheese
- ½ cup pizza sauce

DIRECTIONS

Preheat oven to 375 degrees F. Line a baking sheet with parchment paper or a silicone baking mat.

In a mixing bowl, combine the breadstick mix, 1 cup Parmesan, eggs, 2 Tbsp. olive oil and water. Mix until it just begins to form a dough; it is OK if the dough is crumbly. Dump the mixture out onto a clean work surface and knead until smooth.

Roll the dough into a rectangle 8 inches by 16 inches. Cut the dough into 2- by 8-inch strips.

Cut the cheese into thin strips and divide among the dough, laying on top. Brush some water on the edges of the dough and seal. Roll the dough gently to make round logs. Place the breadsticks on the prepared baking sheet. Brush the tops of the breadsticks with olive oil and sprinkle with the remaining Parmesan cheese. Bake for 20 to 25 minutes or until golden brown.

Serve warm with pizza sauce if desired.

DID YOU KNOW?

John Wayne's 1957 adventure film *Legend of the Lost* had the American actor working in Italy with bombshell Sophia Loren, combining the best of both countries—just like this recipe!

HAM AND CHEESE SANDWICH BALLS

Once you try these hearty bites you might have a tough time saving some for your guests.

MAKES 20

SUPPLIES

- 1 (7.5-oz.) box bread mix
- 2 Tbsp. olive or vegetable oil
- 3 large eggs, divided
- 1 cup shredded sharp cheddar cheese
- 1 cup diced ham
- 2 Tbsp. grainy mustard
- ¼ cup plus 1 Tbsp. water
- 1 tsp. kosher or coarse salt
- 1 tsp. dried onion

DIRECTIONS

Preheat oven to 375 degrees F. Line a baking sheet with parchment paper or a silicone baking mat.

In a large bowl, combine the bread mix, oil, 2 eggs, cheese, ham, mustard and ¼ cup water. Dump the mixture onto a clean work surface and knead until the dough is smooth. Divide the mixture into 20 equal-sized balls. Place the balls on the prepared baking sheet.

Whisk the remaining egg with 1 Tbsp. water. Brush the balls with the egg mixture. Combine the salt and dried onion and sprinkle on top of the balls. Bake for 18 to 20 minutes or until golden brown. Serve immediately.

WAYNE FAMILY TIP

If you want to give these morsels a little more kick, substitute habanero cheddar for the sharp cheddar cheese.

Ethan takes a shot at the toughest guy around—his father. Duke and stuntman Yakima Canutt developed a new system of stunt fighting that looked great on-screen while sparing the actors the worst of bruises.

JALAPEÑO POPPERS

It's tough to decide what's easiest about this snack food—putting it together, or eating them all in one sitting.

MAKES 40 POPPERS

SUPPLIES

- 1 lb. jalapeño peppers
- 8 oz. cream cheese, at room temperature
- 2 cups grated sharp cheddar cheese
- ¼ cup mayonnaise
- 2 large eggs
- 1¼ cups panko style bread crumbs
- 1 tsp. kosher or fine sea salt

DIRECTIONS

Preheat oven to 350 degrees F. Line a baking sheet with parchment paper or a silicone baking mat.

Cut the peppers in half lengthwise. Scrape out the seeds and veins and discard.

In a mixing bowl, combine the cream cheese, cheddar cheese and mayonnaise. Stuff the peppers with the cheese mixture.

Whisk the eggs with 1 tsp. water in a shallow bowl. Pour the breadcrumbs onto a plate and mix in the salt. Dip the peppers into the egg mixture, let the excess drain off, then dip into the breadcrumbs and coat well. Place on the prepared baking sheet.

Spray the tops of the peppers with cooking spray and cook for 30 minutes or until golden brown. Serve warm. Can be reheated in a 350 degree F oven for about 10 minutes.

WAYNE
FAMILY TIP

It might save you time (and bandages) to invest in a pepper-corer rather than using a knife. The curved utensils are less than $10 at most home goods stores.

SEASIDE BAKED CRAB DIP

Living by the ocean means enjoying the bounty of the sea, such as this crab-meat focused favorite.

SERVES 10–12

SUPPLIES

- 8 oz. cream cheese, at room temperature
- ½ cup mayonnaise
- 1½ tsp. seafood seasoning (such as Old Bay)
- 1 lemon, juiced
- 16 oz. canned crabmeat, rinsed and drained
- Kosher or sea salt and pepper, to taste

DIRECTIONS

Preheat oven to 400 degrees F. In a mixing bowl, stir together the cream cheese and mayonnaise until smooth.

Add the seafood seasoning and lemon juice and stir well. Fold in the crabmeat. Season to taste with salt and pepper. (Can be made 1 day ahead and stored, covered with plastic wrap, in the refrigerator.)

Put the dip in an oven-safe baking dish and bake until hot and the top is browned, about 15 minutes. Serve warm with endive leaves, vegetables or crackers.

DID YOU KNOW?
In 1943, Duke went to the South Pacific to support the troops by visiting injured soldiers in hospitals and putting on USO shows for the brave men fighting in WWII.

55

SPICY CHICKEN WINGS

If you and yours share Duke's unabashed love for all things spicy and hot, these wings are for you.

SERVES 8–10

SUPPLIES

- 3 lb. chicken wings
- 2 Tbsp. olive oil
- 2 garlic cloves, minced
- 1 (1-in.) piece of fresh ginger, finely grated
- 1 tsp. salt
- ½ tsp. pepper
- ⅓ cup peanut butter
- 2 limes, juiced and zested
- 1 Tbsp. honey
- 1-2 Tbsp. chili garlic sauce
- 2 tsp. fish sauce
- 1 tsp. toasted sesame seeds

DIRECTIONS

Preheat oven to 425 degrees F. In a large mixing bowl, whisk together the oil, garlic, ginger, salt and pepper. Add the chicken wings and toss to coat. Arrange the wings on a rimmed baking sheet in a single layer. Bake for 30 minutes.

While the chicken wings are baking, combine the peanut butter, lime juice, lime zest, honey, chili garlic sauce and fish sauce in a small sauce pan. Heat over medium and cook until the mixture is smooth and combined.

After the wings have cooked for 30 minutes, drain off any juices from the pan. Brush half the sauce on the wings, bake for 10 minutes, flip the wings and brush with the remaining sauce. Cook for another 10 minutes. Sprinkle with sesame seeds and serve.

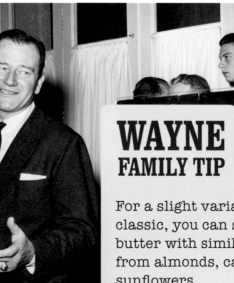

WAYNE FAMILY TIP

For a slight variation on this classic, you can substitute peanut butter with similar products from almonds, cashews or even sunflowers.

CHOCOLATE-COVERED PRETZELS

Looking for a way to make pretzels even better? Just add chocolate.

SERVES 10–12

SUPPLIES

- 1 (14-oz.) bag pretzel twists
- 1 cup semi-sweet chocolate chips
- 1 cup chopped slivered almonds

DIRECTIONS

Line 2 baking sheets with parchment or waxed paper. Place the pretzels on the paper close to each other, saving any broken pretzels for another use.

Melt the chocolate chips in a microwave or in a bowl over barely simmering water until most of the chips are melted (1 to 1 ½ minutes in the microwave), then stir until smooth and glossy. Scrape the chocolate into a small plastic food storage bag. Cut off the tip of one of the corners of the bag and drizzle the chocolate back and forth over the pretzels. Sprinkle the chocolate with the chopped almonds.

Transfer the baking sheets to the refrigerator for 1 hour or until the chocolate is firm. (Can be made 1 day ahead and stored in a covered container in the refrigerator.)

DID YOU KNOW?

John Wayne was a big fan of after-school snacks and spending time with his children. "A lot of times he'd pick me up from school. We would walk around town and go to Sears," Marisa says, adding that trips usually ended with popcorn or ice cream.

PERFECT PICO de GALLO

Sure, you can buy salsa from a store somewhere, but there's nothing better than the satisfaction that comes with creating something on your own.

SERVES 6

SUPPLIES

12 Roma tomatoes, seeded and chopped

1 large white onion, finely diced

3-4 jalapeño or serrano peppers, seeds and veins removed, finely minced

2 cups chopped fresh cilantro, stems removed

2 limes, juiced

Kosher salt and pepper, to taste

DIRECTIONS

Combine the tomatoes, onion, jalapeño or serrano peppers and cilantro in a large mixing bowl and stir to combine. Add the lime juice and stir to combine. Add salt and pepper to taste.

WAYNE
FAMILY TIP

Pep up your pico by adding serranos or chipotles to your jalapeño pepper mix.

Michael Wayne and Duke soak in some sun in Hawaii. Michael produced many of his father's films and later went on to found John Wayne Enterprises to protect and promote the icon's legacy.

BBQ WINGS WITH DIPPING SAUCE

The next time you have everyone gathered to watch the big game, score a win by serving these mouth-watering wings.

SERVES 6

SUPPLIES

Wings

16 oz. Italian dressing

1 (7-oz.) can chipotle peppers in adobo sauce

3 garlic cloves

20–25 chicken wings

Salt and pepper, to taste

Barbecue sauce, as needed

Dipping Sauce

½ cup sour cream

1 Tbsp. extra-virgin olive oil

2 ½ oz. (½ package) Boursin cheese (garlic and herb flavor)

DIRECTIONS

Combine the Italian dressing, entire contents of the can of peppers and the garlic in a food processor. Process to combine well. Rinse your chicken wings and lay them flat. Season with salt and pepper and put into a large plastic food storage bag.

Pour the marinade over the wings and seal the bag. Swish the marinade around the wings to ensure an even coating. Refrigerate for 30 to 45 minutes.

Fire up your grill: Set the temperature to 325 degrees F if you have a gas grill. If you have a charcoal grill, set your grill up for indirect heat. While you are cooking your wings you will want to have both the top and bottom vents open and the lid on.

Place the wings on indirect heat and cook for 12 minutes, then flip the wings and cook for another 12 minutes. Flip the wings and cook for another 12 minutes, then flip again. Brush the wings very thickly with barbecue sauce and cook for 6 minutes. Flip the wings. Brush very thickly with more barbecue sauce and cook for another 6 minutes.

To make the dipping sauce, place all of the ingredients for the sauce in a food processor. Process until well blended. Serve with the wings.

WAYNE FAMILY TIP

Cooking wings without sauce and serving them with different dips gives your guests a choice of flavors.

Lighter Fare

During the middle of the day, you just want something delicious that won't weigh you down. Fortunately, none of these recipes skimp on taste.

CHISUM'S BARBECUE BEAN CHILI

This recipe will leave even the hungriest and grizzled of trail hands with a full belly and full smile.

SERVES 8

SUPPLIES

- 1 lb. dried small red beans
- 1 lb. lean ground beef
- 2 yellow onions, peeled and diced
- 6 garlic cloves, peeled and chopped
- 4 ripe tomatoes, chopped
- 1 cup fresh or frozen white corn
- 1 cup barbecue sauce
- ¼ cup minced fresh cilantro
- 2 Tbsp. chili powder
- 1 Tbsp. ground cumin
- 1 cup chicken broth

DIRECTIONS

Add the beans to a pot with water to cover and cook for 10 minutes at a rapid boil. Let the beans sit in the hot water for 1 hour before draining and placing into the insert of a 6-quart slow cooker. (Red beans must be boiled before putting into the slow cooker to remove a naturally occurring potential toxin.)

In a large skillet over medium heat, cook the beef, onions and garlic, stirring, until the meat has browned. Drain off any accumulated fat. Transfer to the insert. Add the tomatoes, corn, barbecue sauce, cilantro, chili powder and cumin. Stir in the broth.

Cover and cook on low for 8 to 10 hours or on high for about 5 hours. The chili is finished when the beans have reached desired tenderness and have begun to split. If you live at high elevation, add an additional 3 hours to the cooking time.

DID YOU KNOW?

The movie *Chisum* (1970) is loosely based on the real-life Lincoln County Cattle War, a conflict between businessmen in 19th-century New Mexico.

RICH AND TASTY VEGETABLE SOUP

When you want a bowl of something delicious and filling, this soup fits the bill.

SERVES 6–8

SUPPLIES

- 4 slices bacon
- 1½ cups diced onion
- 2 cups sliced carrots, cut into ½-inch chunks
- 2½ cups diced butternut squash, peeled and cut into ½-inch chunks
- 4 garlic cloves, chopped
- 4 thyme sprigs
- 1 (28-oz.) can crushed tomatoes in puree
- 6 cups chicken broth
- 2 tsp. kosher or fine sea salt
- 1 tsp. pepper
- ½ tsp. crushed red pepper flakes
- 2 bay leaves
- 8 oz. penne
- 1 (15.5-oz) can cannellini beans, drained and rinsed
- 5 oz. spinach leaves
- 4 slices sandwich bread (each slice about ½-inch thick)
- 3 Tbsp. basil pesto
- 2 Tbsp. olive oil
- Parmesan cheese (optional)

DIRECTIONS

Chop the bacon and put into a large, cold stockpot. Turn heat to medium and cook the bacon, stirring occasionally, until the bacon fat is rendered and the bacon is starting to brown, about 6 minutes. Add the onions, carrots, squash, garlic and thyme sprigs. Cook over medium heat until the onions are softened, about 8 minutes. Add the tomatoes, chicken broth, salt, pepper, red pepper flakes and bay leaves. Raise heat to high, bring to a boil then reduce heat and simmer, uncovered, for 30 minutes or until the vegetables are fork tender.

While the soup is simmering, bring a large pot of heavily salted water to a boil. Add the penne and cook according to the package directions. Drain the pasta and rinse under hot water.

Make the croutons: Preheat oven to 400 degrees F. Cut the bread into cubes (9 cubes per slice of bread). In a mixing bowl, combine the pesto and olive oil. Add the breadcrumbs and toss gently until the bread is fully coated. Lay in a single layer on a baking sheet and cook for 10 minutes.

Once the soup has simmered for 30 minutes and the veggies are tender, remove the bay leaves and thyme sprigs, add the pasta and beans and heat through. Add the spinach and stir into the soup. Cook just until the spinach is wilted.

To serve, ladle the soup into bowls, top with some croutons and a grating of Parmesan cheese, if desired.

WAYNE
FAMILY TIP

Good things take time, including this soup. For optimal flavor, don't rush. Let the soup simmer for the allotted time—or longer!

RIO BRAVO BLACK BEAN SOUP

Just like Duke's Sheriff John T. Chance assembled a great team to get the job done, this soup brings together a whole heap of ingredients to guarantee you'll put something tasty in your mouth.

SERVES 6–8

SUPPLIES

Soup

- 1 package black bean soup mix
- 2 Tbsp. olive oil
- 1 medium yellow or white onion, chopped
- 2 red bell peppers, seeded and chopped
- 1 jalapeño pepper, seeds and veins removed, minced
- 8 cups water
- 2 whole oranges
- ½ cup taco sauce
- 1 tsp. kosher or fine sea salt
- ½ tsp. pepper
- A few dashes of hot pepper sauce, to taste

Salsa

- 4 medium oranges, peeled and cut into segments
- ¼ medium red onion, thinly sliced
- 1 small jalapeño, seeds and veins removed and finely minced
- ¼ cup fresh cilantro
- 1 lime, juiced
- 1 tsp. honey

DIRECTIONS

Soup

Soak the beans for 8 to 24 hours in enough water to cover the beans by a couple of inches. Reserve the seasoning packet.

Drain and rinse the beans. Heat the olive oil in a large soup pan or Dutch oven over medium-high. Add the onions, red pepper and jalapeño, and sauté for about 5 minutes or until the veggies are soft. Add the drained beans and water. Grate the zest of the oranges into the pot with a microplane or other fine grater.

Raise the heat, bring to a boil, reduce heat, cover the pot and simmer for 2 hours. Remove the lid, add the reserved flavor packet, taco sauce, 1 tsp. of salt, ½ tsp. of pepper and hot sauce. Let cook for another 30 minutes uncovered or until the soup is the consistency you like.

Serve with tortilla chips, sour cream, citrus salsa and cilantro leaves, if desired.

Citrus Salsa

In a small mixing bowl, combine the orange segments, red onion, jalapeño, cilantro, lime juice and honey. Serve with the soup.

WAYNE
FAMILY TIP

If you like it hot, leave the jalapeño seeds in! They'll greatly increase the heat in your dish.

BIG JAKE'S CHICKEN AND DUMPLINGS

This old-school recipe is a quick and easy way to ensure your family will always look forward to mealtime.

SERVES 6–8

SUPPLIES

- 2 Tbsp. olive oil
- 3 medium carrots, diced
- 1 large onion, diced
- 2 garlic cloves, minced
- 8 cups chicken broth
- 1 whole rotisserie chicken, skin and bones removed and shredded or chopped
- 2 bay leaves
- 6 slices bacon
- 1 lb. mushrooms, cleaned and sliced
- 4 green onions, white and green parts chopped
- Kosher salt and pepper, to taste
- 1½ cups flour
- 1 tsp. baking powder
- ½ tsp. baking soda
- 1½ tsp. sugar
- 2 Tbsp. butter, melted
- 1 cup (more or less) buttermilk

DIRECTIONS

In a large soup pot or Dutch oven, heat the olive oil over medium-high. Add the carrots and onion and cook until softened, about 5 minutes. Add the garlic and cook for another 30 seconds. Add the chicken broth, chicken and bay leaves and bring to a gentle boil. Reduce the heat and let simmer for 15 minutes.

While the soup is simmering, chop the bacon into ½-inch pieces. Place in a large skillet and cook over medium heat until it has rendered its fat and the bacon is crispy. Remove the bacon pieces with a slotted spoon, and add the mushrooms. Raise the heat to medium-high and cook the mushrooms, stirring occasionally, until they are browned, about 8 minutes. Take off the heat, add the bacon back to the pan and add the green onions. Season to taste with salt and pepper and reserve until you serve the chicken and dumplings.

In a mixing bowl, whisk together the flour, baking powder, baking soda, ¾ tsp. salt and sugar. Add the melted butter and stir with a fork. Starting with about ¾ cup, stir in the buttermilk. Keep adding buttermilk, a little at a time, until the mixture forms into a soft dough.

Drop tablespoons of the batter onto the top of the simmering soup, cover the pan and let simmer for 15 minutes.

Serve in bowls topped with the bacon mixture.

DID YOU KNOW?

In the movie *Big Jake* (1971), John Wayne shares the screen with two of his sons—Patrick and Ethan— making it a true family affair!

75

TURKEY BEAN SOUP

This soup is so chock-full of hearty goodness, you'll barely be able to drag your spoon through it!

SERVES 10–12

SUPPLIES

Soup

- 1 package black bean soup mix
- 1 onion, diced
- 1 (1-lb.) bag fresh or frozen corn kernels
- 1 (14.5-oz.) can diced tomatoes, drained
- 1 (4-oz.) can diced mild green chilies
- 1 bunch green onions, sliced
- ½ tsp. kosher or fine sea salt
- ½ tsp. pepper
- 1 tsp. garlic powder
- 4 cups cooked turkey or chicken, shredded
- Sour cream (recipe follows)
- Handful of cilantro leaves

Sour Cream

- 1 cup sour cream
- 1-3 tsp. pureed chipotle in adobo depending on heat level you like
- 1 lime, juiced and zested, zest finely grated

DIRECTIONS

Soup

Remove the flavor packet from the beans and save. Place the beans in a large soup pot and cover with water. Let sit, covered, overnight or for at least 8 hours. Drain the water from the beans. Place back in the pot and add 8 cups of cold water along with the reserved flavor packet.

Bring to a boil, cover and let simmer for 90 minutes to 2 hours or until the beans are tender. Add the corn, tomatoes, chilies, green onions, salt, pepper, garlic powder and turkey or chicken and heat through, 5 to 10 minutes. Taste and add more salt and pepper if needed.

Serve with sour cream and cilantro for garnish.

Sour Cream

Stir the ingredients together and let sit covered in the refrigerator until time to serve.

WAYNE FAMILY TIP

Soup doesn't just have to be one meal. Double the recipe and freeze it, so you can have it for lunch and maybe even dinner in a few days.

SPLIT PEA SOUP

This delicious and delightful soup will keep you warm no matter what the weather is outside.

SERVES 6

SUPPLIES

- 1 Tbsp. olive oil
- 1 medium white or yellow onion, chopped
- 2-3 medium carrots, peeled and diced
- 3 cloves garlic, minced
- 1 package split pea soup mix
- 7 cups water
- 5-6 dashes hot sauce
- 1 lemon, juiced
- Salt and pepper, if needed
- 4 strips bacon
- 4 green onions, sliced thinly

DIRECTIONS

Heat olive oil in a soup pan or Dutch oven over medium-high. Add the onions and carrots and sauté until the onions are translucent, about 5 to 6 minutes. Add the garlic and cook for 30 seconds. Rinse and drain the split peas and add to the pot along with the seasoning packet and water. Bring to a boil, reduce heat, cover pan and simmer for 45 minutes. Add hot sauce, lemon juice and some salt and pepper to taste, if needed. Cook for 10 more minutes.

While the soup is cooking, cut the bacon into small, ¼-inch pieces. Put into a cold frying pan; turn on the heat to medium and cook, stirring often until the bacon is very browned and crispy. Transfer to a plate lined with paper towels and drain well.

Serve soup garnished with bacon bits and green onions.

WAYNE FAMILY TIP

As an alternative, try swapping out the bacon for sliced kosher hot dogs.

Duke spends some well-deserved downtime with a book. While the Western legend loved stories about cowboys, he also enjoyed the work of Sir Arthur Conan Doyle, the creator of Sherlock Holmes.

CORN AND BACON PASTA

Corn, bacon and pasta—it's the holy trinity of crowd-pleasing food finally brought together in one recipe. Get to it and enjoy the praise from your loved ones.

SERVES 4

SUPPLIES

- 8 oz. penne
- 4 slices bacon
- 4 cups fresh corn kernels
- 2 garlic cloves, minced or grated
- ¼ cup sun-dried tomatoes in oil, dried and chopped
- 1 pinch crushed red pepper flakes
- Kosher salt and pepper, to taste
- 1 cup roughly chopped or torn fresh basil leaves
- ½ cup grated Parmesan cheese

DIRECTIONS

Bring a large pot of heavily salted water to a boil and cook the pasta according to the package directions. Reserve about ½ cup of the starchy pasta cooking water and drain the pasta. While the pasta is cooking, cut the bacon in half lengthwise then into ¼-inch pieces. Place in a large skillet and cook over medium heat until browned, about 8 minutes.

Remove the bacon with a slotted spoon and drain on paper towels. Pour off all but 1 Tbsp. of the bacon fat. Add the corn to the hot bacon fat and cook until the corn is tender, about 5 minutes. Add the garlic, sun-dried tomatoes and red pepper flakes and cook for another minute. Add the pasta and about half the pasta cooking water, cook for another minute or two until the sauce comes together, adding more cooking water if it looks too dry.

Remove from heat and stir in the reserved bacon and the basil. Season to taste with salt and pepper. Serve topped with grated Parmesan, if desired.

WAYNE FAMILY TIP

If you're not a fan of sun-dried tomatoes, roasted red peppers would make for an easy, delicious swap.

GRILLED CORN SALAD

Make this dish once, and you'll have the whole family counting the days until corn is back in season.

SERVES 6

SUPPLIES

- 6 ears of corn, husks and silk removed
- Vegetable oil, for brushing
- ¾ tsp. kosher or fine sea salt, plus more for seasoning
- ½ tsp. pepper, plus more for seasoning
- 1 Tbsp. balsamic vinegar
- 2 Tbsp. extra-virgin olive oil
- 1 tsp. Herbes de Provence
- 1 cup fresh basil leaves, packed
- 1 pint grape or cherry tomatoes, halved

DIRECTIONS

Brush the corn with vegetable oil and season with salt and pepper. Place on a grill or grill pan over medium heat. Cook for 8 minutes, turning a quarter turn every 2 minutes. Remove from the grill and let cool.

In a large mixing bowl, whisk together the vinegar, olive oil, ¾ tsp. salt, ½ tsp. pepper and the Herbes de Provence. Cut the corn kernels from the cobs. Add to the dressing along with the tomatoes and stir to combine. Stack the basil leaves on top of each other. Roll up like a cigar and cut with a very sharp knife into thin ribbons. Add the basil to the corn and tomato mixture and stir. Serve immediately or cover with plastic wrap and refrigerate.

DID YOU KNOW?

Although John Wayne spent the majority of his life in California, he was born in Winterset, Iowa, on May 26, 1907. He lived in the Hawkeye State until 1914.

EASTERN COBB SALAD

Duke was never afraid to take a risk or try something new, and you should follow in his footsteps by serving this Asian-influenced salad tonight—you won't regret it.

SERVES 4

SUPPLIES

1 cup sesame salad dressing, divided

3 Tbsp. honey

1 lb. boneless skinless chicken breasts

Kosher or fine sea salt and pepper, for seasoning

1 Tbsp. olive or vegetable oil

6 cups shredded Napa cabbage

2 cups shredded romaine lettuce

2 cups shredded carrots

1 red bell pepper, cored, seeded and finely sliced

1 bunch green onions, thinly sliced on the diagonal

1 English (hothouse) cucumber, halved lengthwise and thinly sliced

1 tsp. sesame seeds

¼ cup cilantro leaves

DIRECTIONS

Combine ½ cup of the dressing with the honey and place in a large plastic food storage bag. Add the chicken breasts, toss to coat and marinate in the refrigerator for 30 minutes to 12 hours.

Remove chicken breast from the refrigerator and discard the marinade. Pat the breasts dry with paper towels and season with salt and pepper. Heat a large skillet over medium-high and coat the bottom of the pan with the oil. Add the chicken breasts; cook for 2 minutes or until golden brown, flip and cook for another 2 minutes. Cover the pan; lower the heat to medium and cook for another 4 to 8 minutes depending on the thickness of the chicken breasts. Let sit for 5 to 10 minutes then slice thinly.

Combine the Napa cabbage with the romaine and place in a layer on a large platter. Arrange the chicken slices, carrots, red pepper, green onions and cucumbers on top of the cabbage/lettuce mixture in rows. Sprinkle with a little more salt and pepper, the sesame seeds, the remaining dressing and cilantro leaves. Serve immediately.

WAYNE
FAMILY TIP

Napa cabbage is also referred to as Chinese cabbage. When picking it out at the store, avoid any heads with limp stems or wilted leaves.

John Wayne and son Patrick on the set of *Rio Grande* (1950). Patrick would become an accomplished actor in his own right, starring alongside his father in multiple films.

KICKIN' CHICKEN STEW

This straightforward stew is chock-full of flavor for the whole family.

SERVES 6

SUPPLIES

- 2 lb. boneless, skinless chicken thighs
- 1 medium onion, sliced
- 6 whole garlic cloves, peeled
- 1 cauliflower head, florets separated
- 2 medium zucchini, sliced
- 1 (15-oz.) can diced tomatoes
- 1 tsp. ground cumin
- 1 tsp. ground coriander
- ½ tsp. turmeric
- ½ tsp. kosher salt
- ½ tsp. cayenne pepper
- 2 cups chicken broth

DIRECTIONS

Use a 6-quart slow cooker. Put the chicken into the bottom of your cooker. Add the onion and whole garlic cloves. Toss the cauliflower and zucchini on top and pour in the tomatoes. Add all of the spices and stir in the chicken broth, taking care to not crumble the cauliflower. Cover and cook on low for 6 to 8 hours, or on high for about 5 hours.

WAYNE
FAMILY TIP

If you choose to freeze this stew, use gallon freezer bags. They'll defrost quickly and stack easily in your freezer!

SWEET POTATO BISQUE

Putting together a pot of this nourishing soup means good times ahead for you and your family.

SERVES 6

SUPPLIES

- 1 Tbsp. olive oil
- 1 medium onion, diced
- 1 medium leek, white and light green parts thinly sliced
- 1 garlic clove, minced
- 1 (4-oz.) can mild green chilies, drained
- 3 medium sweet potatoes, peeled and diced
- 4 cups chicken broth
- ½ cup peanut butter
- Salt and pepper, to taste
- ½ cup chopped cilantro leaves

DIRECTIONS

In a Dutch oven or soup pan, heat the oil over medium. Add the onions and leeks and cook until soft, about 5 minutes. Add the garlic and chilies and cook for another minute. Add the sweet potatoes, chicken broth and peanut butter, raise heat and bring to a boil. Reduce the heat, cover the pan and let simmer until the sweet potatoes are tender, about 20 minutes.

Blend in batches in the blender until smooth. Season to taste with salt and pepper.

Serve garnished with cilantro leaves.

WAYNE FAMILY TIP

If you're looking for a side for the soup, warm up some Texas toast in the oven. It's perfect for soaking up the last few drops of your portion.

John Wayne, and sons Ethan and Patrick spend some quality time on the open water. Duke's favorite boat, the *Wild Goose*, was the setting for countless meals and memories.

MEXICAN CHICKEN NOODLE SOUP

Every mouthful is a fiesta for your tastebuds when you're enjoying this spicy soup.

SERVES 6

SUPPLIES

8 oz. penne

2 Tbsp. olive oil

1 cup chopped red onion

1 cup sliced carrots

2 garlic cloves, minced

1 jalapeño pepper, sliced

2 Tbsp. chili powder, plus more to taste

1½ tsp. ground cumin

1½ tsp. kosher salt

¾ tsp. pepper

6 cups chicken stock

2-3 cups cooked chicken, shredded or chopped

2 cups fresh or frozen corn kernels (thawed if frozen)

DIRECTIONS

Bring a large pot of salted water to a boil. Add the pasta and cook according to the package directions. Drain, rinse with hot water and set aside.

While the pasta is cooking, heat a soup pan or Dutch oven over medium-high. Add the oil, onions and carrots, then cook, stirring occasionally, until the vegetables are soft and just beginning to brown.

Add the garlic, jalapeño slices, chili powder, ground cumin, salt and pepper and cook for 30 seconds, stirring. Add the chicken broth, bring to a boil, reduce the heat and let simmer for 10 minutes. Add the chicken and corn and heat for 2 to 3 minutes.

WAYNE FAMILY TIP

Acidic ingredients are great for brightening up a soup's flavor. Try a squeeze of lime juice for some extra zip!

Main Dishes

Nothing brought a smile to John Wayne's face like the sight of a plate piled high with delicious, filling food. These recipes will have you and yours grinning in no time.

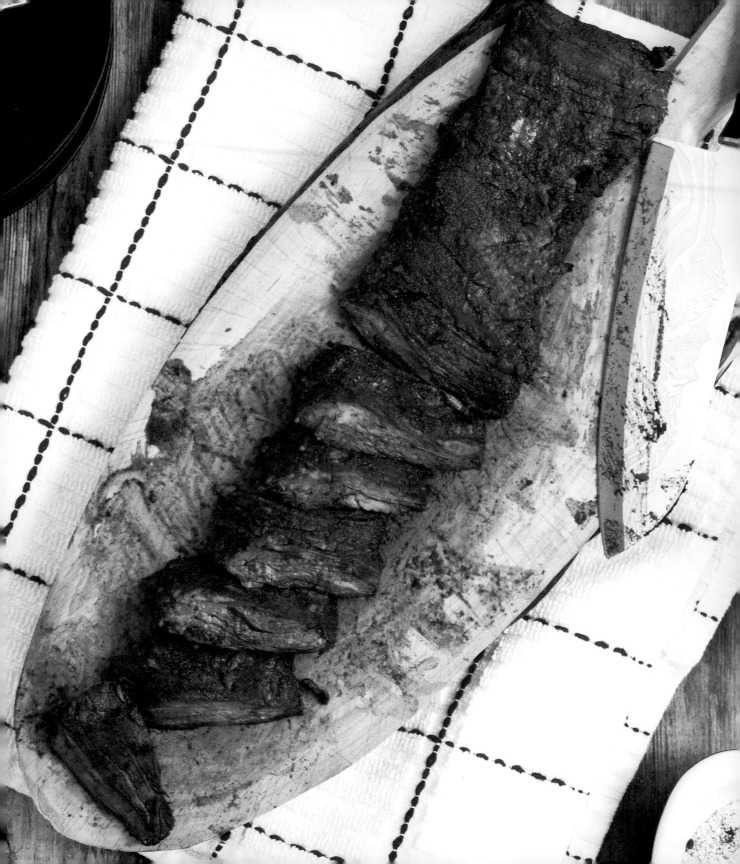

SPICY GRILLED SKIRT STEAK

It's hard to improve upon the beauty of a well-grilled steak, but this recipe manages the impossible task with no muss or fuss.

SERVES 6

SUPPLIES

- 4 Tbsp. brown sugar
- 2 Tbsp. kosher salt
- 2 Tbsp. smoked paprika
- 1 Tbsp. garlic powder
- 2 tsp. cayenne pepper
- 2 ½ lb. skirt steak
- Vegetable oil
- ¼ cup butter, melted

DIRECTIONS

In a small mixing bowl, combine the brown sugar, salt, paprika, garlic powder and cayenne pepper. Press the mixture generously on both sides of the skirt steak. Let sit at room temperature while preparing the grill.

Prepare the grill for direct heat. Brush the grill grates with oil.

Pat the steak dry and grill for 2 to 3 minutes per side for medium rare. Cover the steak with foil and let sit for 10 minutes before slicing.

If using a grill pan, heat the pan until it is screaming hot, do not oil the pan, and grill as above.

DID YOU KNOW ?
Duke always had his steaks "charred medium," and ate them with his own brand of steak sauce.

LENTILS AND SAUSAGE

It doesn't matter how hungry they are—this hearty dish will keep them satisfied.

SERVES 6–8

SUPPLIES

- 2 Tbsp. olive oil
- 1 white or yellow onion, chopped
- 2 carrots, diced
- 1 celery rib, diced
- 3 garlic cloves, minced
- 1 package lentil soup mix
- 6 cups water
- 1 bunch kale, ribs removed, leaves coarsely chopped
- 2 Tbsp. balsamic vinegar
- Hot sauce, to taste
- Kosher salt and pepper, to taste
- 4 Italian sausages

DIRECTIONS

In a large Dutch oven or soup pot, heat the olive oil over medium-high. Add the onions, carrots and celery and cook until they start to soften, about 5 minutes. Add the garlic and cook for 30 seconds.

Rinse and pick over the lentils. Add to the pot along with the enclosed seasoning packet and 6 cups water. Bring to a boil, cover the pan, reduce heat to low and simmer for 30 minutes.

Heat a medium skillet over medium-high. Prick the skins of the Italian sausage and brown the sausages on all sides, about 5 to 6 minutes. Add about ¼ inch of water to the skillet, cover the skillet and reduce heat to medium. Cook until the sausages are cooked through, 10 to 15 minutes. Cover with foil to keep warm.

After the lentils have simmered for 30 minutes, remove the cover on the pan, stir in the kale and vinegar and cook until the kale is wilted and the lentils are tender, about 10 minutes. If you want your lentils soupier, you can add more water. Taste the lentils and season with salt, pepper and hot sauce. Slice the sausages on the diagonal and serve on top of the lentils.

DID YOU KNOW?

Dinner was one of Duke's favorite times of the day. He loved getting his entire family—and friends—together for a meal in his Newport Beach home.

TACOS

Need inspiration for your next Taco Tuesday? Look East and leave your family with their jaws hanging.

SERVES 12

SUPPLIES

- 1½ lb. skirt steak
- ⅔ cup soy sauce
- 6 Tbsp. Mirin
- 6 Tbsp. brown sugar
- 2 Tbsp. sesame oil
- 4 garlic cloves, minced
- 4 green onions, finely chopped
- 2 tsp. grated fresh ginger
- 12 corn tortillas
- 12 lettuce leaves

DIRECTIONS

Place the steak in a large food storage bag. Combine the soy sauce, Mirin, brown sugar, sesame oil, garlic, green onions and ginger in a mixing bowl. Whisk to combine. Pour the marinade over the meat and let sit at room temperature for 30 minutes. (If making ahead, you can marinate it in the refrigerator for up to 24 hours.)

Heat a grill or grill pan to medium-high.

Pat the steak dry with paper towels and grill 2 minutes per side. Let rest for 10 minutes then slice thinly.

Grill the tortillas 30 to 60 seconds per side. Keep warm.

To serve, place a lettuce leaf on top of a tortilla and top with some sliced meat.

WAYNE FAMILY TIP

You can use any lettuce you have on hand, but Bibb lettuce works best for these tacos.

EASY-TO-MAKE EGGPLANT LASAGNA

Don't put off cooking this can't-miss lasagna recipe for another moment—trust us, your family will thank you.

SERVES 8–10

SUPPLIES

- 2 medium or large eggplants
- ¾ cup olive oil
- 5 tsp. dried oregano, divided
- 3 tsp. kosher or sea salt, divided
- 2 tsp. pepper, divided
- 5 cups tomato sauce
- 1½ lb. Italian sausage
- 1 large white or yellow onion, chopped
- 3 garlic cloves, minced
- 1 large container ricotta cheese
- 1 cup Parmesan cheese, grated or shredded
- 2 large eggs, beaten
- 2 tsp. dried parsley
- 3 cups mozzarella cheese, grated

WAYNE FAMILY TIP

To avoid bitter eggplant, generously salt the slices before cooking. Let sit for 30 minutes, then rinse and pat dry.

DIRECTIONS

Preheat oven to 350 degrees F.

Mix olive oil with 2 tsp. dried oregano, 2 tsp. salt and 1 tsp. pepper. Cut the ends off the eggplant and slice into ¼-inch slices. Brush eggplant slices with olive oil mixture. Grill on a hot, dry grill pan or broil under pre-heated broiler for about 4 to 5 minutes (until browned) and flip, cook on other side until browned and slightly soft about another 3 to 4 minutes. It will cook more in the oven so slightly undercooked is OK. Set aside time to layer the lasagna.

Remove the casing from the Italian sausage and crumble into a large stockpot or skillet that has been heated over medium-high. Add chopped onion and cook until soft, about 5 minutes. Add the garlic and cook another 30 seconds. Add tomato sauce, wine if using and 1 tsp. dried oregano. Let cook for about 15 minutes until heated through.

In a large mixing bowl, mix the ricotta cheese with 1 tsp. salt, 1 tsp. pepper, 2 tsp. dried oregano, the parsley, 1 cup Parmesan cheese and eggs.

Brush a large lasagna dish with some olive oil. Ladle in a little bit of the tomato sauce and

spread over bottom of dish. Try to just add the sauce—no sausage chunks.

Layer half the eggplant slices in the bottom. Add half the ricotta mixture, then top with half

the sauce. Repeat layering.

Top with mozzarella cheese and spread evenly over the top. Bake about 1 hour until hot and bubbling and cheese is browned.

PERFECT PORK CHOPS

Sometimes, happiness is a plate piled high with pork chops. Go with this recipe tonight and make someone's dream come true.

SERVES 4

SUPPLIES

- 1 cup plus 2 Tbsp. maple syrup, divided
- 1 cup kosher salt
- ¾ cup sugar
- 3 Tbsp. plus 1 tsp. Dijon mustard, divided
- 2 Tbsp. minced fresh rosemary
- 1 tsp. pepper
- 6 cups water
- 2 cups ice
- 4 center-cut loin pork chops (about 1 inch thick)
- Olive oil, for brushing the chops

DIRECTIONS

Combine 1 cup maple syrup, salt, sugar, 3 Tbsp. Dijon mustard, rosemary and pepper with the water in a saucepan. Bring to a boil, stirring to dissolve the sugar and salt. Take off the heat, stir in the ice. Pour the brining liquid into a large plastic storage bag or into a glass baking dish deep enough to hold the chops. Add the chops and refrigerate for between 1 and 12 hours.

Heat a grill pan or skillet over medium until hot. Combine the remaining 2 Tbsp. maple syrup with the remaining tsp. of Dijon mustard.

Remove the chops from the brining liquid, rinse with cold water and pat dry. Sprinkle some pepper on each side of the chops and brush with oil. Place the chops on the hot pan and cook 4 to 5 minutes per side depending on their thickness. Brush the cooked chops with the maple flavored agave nectar/Dijon Mustard sauce. Let them rest for 5 minutes and serve.

WAYNE FAMILY TIP

Before cooking, take the chops out of the fridge and rest them on the counter for about 15 to 30 minutes so they get to room temperature. This prevents the outside from overcooking.

JIM McLAIN'S BIG BEEF BRISKET

Big Jim McLain didn't take any guff from anyone—and neither will this classic recipe in its mission to leave your family full and satisfied.

SERVES 6

SUPPLIES

- 1 tsp. kosher salt
- ½ tsp. pepper
- 1 tsp. powdered garlic
- 1 (3-lb.) beef brisket, trimmed of fat
- 1 large white or yellow onion, thinly sliced
- 12 oz. barbecue sauce
- ½ cup brown sugar
- 1 (10-oz.) can diced tomatoes and chilies, undrained
- 1½ lb. small white potatoes

DIRECTIONS

Preheat oven to 325 degrees F.

Combine the salt, pepper and garlic powder in small bowl and rub all over the brisket. Place in a baking dish. Cover the beef with the sliced onions.

Combine the barbecue sauce, brown sugar, canned tomatoes and chilies. Pour over the beef and cover the dish with foil. Bake for 3 hours. Leave oven on.

Remove the foil, add the potatoes and cook, uncovered for another 40 to 45 minutes or until the potatoes are tender. Let rest for 10 minutes, slice the beef and return to the dish. Spoon the sauce over the beef and serve.

DID YOU KNOW?
Duke's 1952 film *Big Jim McLain* saw John Wayne paired with actor James Arness as investigators hunting communists. Talk about a couple of beefcakes!

Duke and Marisa enjoy time on the Wild Goose. Marisa and her siblings would often spend the days on the boat waterskiing.

TIN STAR TURKEY MEATBALLS

You and yours will always win the showdown against hunger when you serve up this recipe.

SERVES 4

SUPPLIES

- ½ cup breadcrumbs
- 1 tsp. kosher or fine sea salt
- 1 tsp. pepper
- 1 tsp. garlic powder
- 2 Tbsp. dried onion flakes
- ¼ cup parsley, minced
- 1 ½ cups chicken stock, divided
- 1 ¼ lb. ground turkey
- 2 Tbsp. olive oil
- 1 (12-oz.) bag fresh or frozen cranberries (about 2 ½ cups)
- 1 cup orange sauce
- 3 Tbsp. sugar

DIRECTIONS

Preheat oven to 450 degrees F.

Combine the breadcrumbs, salt, pepper, garlic powder, onion flakes, parsley and ½ cup chicken stock in a large mixing bowl and let sit for 5 minutes. Add the turkey and mix with hands until thoroughly combined. Shape into 2-inch balls (about 2 Tbsp. each). Heat the oil in a large skillet over medium-high and sauté the meatballs until browned all over, about 6 minutes. Place browned meatballs on a baking sheet and bake in oven until cooked through, about 10 minutes.

Add the cranberries to the skillet the meatballs were browned in along with the remaining cup of chicken stock, orange sauce and sugar. Cook over medium-high heat until the cranberries pop and the sauce is reduced by half, about 7 minutes. Add the meatballs to the gravy and serve.

DID YOU KNOW?
John Wayne starred with two singing sensations in 1959's *Rio Bravo*—Dean Martin and Ricky Nelson.

TOO-TASTY MEDITERRANEAN CHICKEN

The smell of this chicken recipe cooking in the kitchen will have everyone in the house obsessing over one question—is it ready yet?

SERVES 4

SUPPLIES

- 4 bone-in, skin-on chicken breasts
- 4 Tbsp. olive oil, divided
- Salt and pepper, to taste
- 2 pints grape tomatoes
- 4 large shallots
- 1 small bunch fresh thyme, divided
- 2 (15-oz.) cans white beans, drained and rinsed
- ½ cup chicken broth
- 1 tsp. dried oregano
- 2 Tbsp. chopped fresh Italian flat leaf parsley

DIRECTIONS

Preheat oven to 400 degrees F.

Place chicken breasts on a shallow roasting pan or cookie sheet with sides. Pour on about 2 Tbsp. olive oil, sprinkle generously with salt and pepper and rub all over both sides of the chicken breasts to coat well. Arrange skin side up and put in the upper part of the oven.

Cut tomatoes in half lengthwise. Cut shallots in half from top to root end, remove outer skin and then slice each half into 4 pieces lengthwise. Place tomatoes and shallots in another roasting pan or cookie sheet. Toss with about 1 Tbsp. of oil, salt and pepper. Spread into an even layer. Lay 4 or 5 sprigs of thyme over the tomatoes and shallots. Place in lower part of oven with chicken.

Cook chicken and tomato/shallot mixture for 40 minutes. The chicken should be golden brown and the juices should run clear when pricked with a knife. Tomatoes should be tender and starting to caramelize. Remove thyme sprigs and discard.

Cover chicken with foil and let rest while preparing the beans.

Put beans into a large skillet; add roasted tomatoes and shallots, chicken

WAYNE FAMILY TIP

Feeling extra hungry? Serve this chicken over a bed of rice to make it a meal worth unbuckling your belt for.

broth, oregano and some fresh thyme leaves (about 2 tsp.) pulled from the stems. Cook over medium-high heat until tomatoes start breaking apart and chicken broth is almost all reduced. Will likely be about 5 minutes. Taste for seasoning; add more salt and pepper if desired.

Arrange bean/tomato mixture on a platter and top with chicken breasts. Drizzle with additional olive oil (about 1 Tbsp.) and garnish with chopped fresh parsley.

RED RIVER BRAISED SHORT RIBS

These provisions are worth driving across the country for—with or without cattle.

SERVES 6–8

SUPPLIES

Braised Short Ribs

- 1 tsp. salt
- 1 tsp. pepper
- 2 tsp. garlic powder
- 5 lb. lean short ribs of beef, cut into 3- to 4-inch pieces
- 1 large white onion, diced
- 2 cups mango nectar
- ¾ cup beef broth, divided
- 1-2 chipotle peppers in adobo with some sauce, smashed with

a fork or blended until smooth
- 4 green onions, sliced for garnish

Smashed Potatoes

- 4 lb. Yukon Gold potatoes, cut into 3-inch pieces
- 1 tsp. salt
- ½ tsp. pepper
- ½ stick butter
- 1 cup half-and-half
- 3 Tbsp. heavy cream (optional)

WAYNE
FAMILY TIP

Don't like mango nectar? Switch it out for your favorite barbecue sauce. But trust us—you're missing out.

DIRECTIONS

Braised Short Ribs

Heat a large skillet over medium-high.

Mix together salt, pepper and garlic powder and season short ribs. Brown ribs in batches on all sides until well browned, about 10 minutes per batch. Remove from pan and drain on paper towels. Place ribs in a large Dutch oven or heavy stock pot.

Pour off most of the fat from the skillet leaving about 2 tsp. Sauté the diced onions until translucent but not browned. Add nectar and ½ cup beef broth. Cook for about 1 minute just to meld flavors. Pour over ribs and stir well.

Cover and bake in oven for about 3 hours or until the meat is very tender and almost falling off the bones. Remove from heat and let cool. Cover and refrigerate overnight.

About 30 minutes before serving, remove from fridge and remove and discard the fat that has settled at the top. Add ¼ cup beef broth and smashed chipotle pepper(s) and re-heat on top of the stove over medium heat for about 20 minutes or until heated through. Taste the sauce and add more salt and pepper if needed.

Put a large spoonful or two of smashed potatoes in a shallow soup bowl, top with 2 or 3 ribs, spoon over some sauce and garnish with chopped green onions.

Smashed Potatoes

In a large pot of heavily salted water over high heat, boil potatoes until tender (about 15 to 20 minutes).

Pour off water and return pan with potatoes in it to the high heat and cook for about 2 minutes until the moisture has evaporated. Add salt and pepper and smash potatoes with a potato masher. Add butter, half-and-half and cream if using. Mash some more until the potatoes are chunky not smooth. Taste and add more salt and pepper if needed.

Can be made ahead about 3 hours. Keep at room temp and then reheat over simmering water or in a 350 degree F oven. If reheating in the oven, add 1 to 2 more Tbsp. of butter and about ¼ cup more of half-and-half. Stir well before serving.

COWBOY STEAK AND WHITE BEAN CHILI

The rugged pioneers of the Old West demanded the very best when it came to chow time. So should you, which is why you need to cook this recipe tonight.

SERVES 10–12

SUPPLIES

- 1 (12-oz.) bag bean chili mix
- 1 tsp. kosher or fine sea salt
- ½ tsp. pepper
- 1 tsp. chili powder
- 2 lb. beef round, cut into 1-inch pieces
- 1 Tbsp. olive oil
- 1 large onion, diced
- 2 cloves garlic, minced
- 1-2 Tbsp. chipotle puree*
- 1 (14.5-oz.) can diced tomatoes, undrained
- 6 cups water

   *Create chipotle puree by blending a can of chipotle in adobo sauce in the blender until smooth. Store in a covered jar in the refrigerator for up to 6 months.

DIRECTIONS

Reserve the flavor packet from the bag of beans, cover the beans with at least 2 inches of water and soak for 8 to 24 hours. Drain and rinse.

Combine the salt, pepper and chili powder in a small bowl. Sprinkle the beef with the mixture, coating evenly.

Heat the oil over medium-high in a large stock pot or Dutch oven until hot. Add the beef in 2 batches, cooking each batch until browned on all sides (about 5 to 6 minutes per batch). Remove beef to a plate and reserve. Add the onion to the pan and cook until it softens and starts to brown, about 3 minutes. Add the garlic; cook for 30 seconds then stir in the beef, beans, reserved flavor packet, chipotle puree, canned tomatoes and water. Bring to a boil, cover the pan, reduce to a simmer and cook for 1 hour.

Remove the lid and continue to simmer for another 30 minutes or until the beef and beans are tender and the liquid has reduced down to the thickness you prefer. Taste and adjust seasoning with more salt, pepper or chipotle puree, if desired.

DID YOU KNOW?
Duke had a great love for the cowboy way of life and collected a variety of Western art over the years.

RACK OF LAMB

This tender and tasty recipe will fill your stomach and warm your heart.

SERVES 6

SUPPLIES

- 1 lemon
- 2 racks of lamb (6–8 bones each), trimmed and frenched (have your butcher do this)
- Kosher or fine sea salt and pepper, to taste
- 3 Tbsp. extra-virgin olive oil, divided
- ½ cup shelled, roasted and salted pistachios
- 3 cups fresh mint leaves, loosely packed
- 3 garlic cloves, minced

DIRECTIONS

Preheat oven to 450 degrees F. Zest the lemon with a grater and squeeze the juice. Set aside.

Heat an oven-safe skillet or roasting pan large enough to hold both racks of lamb over medium-high. Season the lamb generously with salt and pepper on all sides. Add 1 Tbsp. of the olive oil to the hot pan and sear the lamb on all sides for about 2 minutes per side. Let cool slightly.

Put the pistachios in a food processor and pulse a few times to grind them. Add the remaining 2 Tbsp. of olive oil and the mint, garlic, lemon zest and lemon juice. Process until it turns into a paste. Spread the paste on the meat side of the lamb, pressing down firmly. Place the racks back into the skillet or pan bone side down and roast for 20 minutes for medium rare or 25 minutes for medium. Remove the lamb from oven. Cover loosely with a piece of foil. Let rest for 10 minutes before cutting the lamb into chops using a thin, sharp knife.

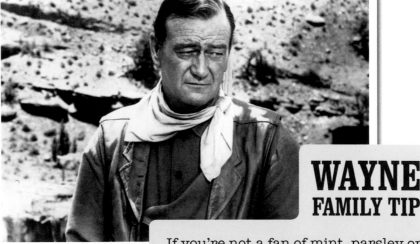

WAYNE
FAMILY TIP

If you're not a fan of mint, parsley or basil can be used instead.

Duke (back row, fourth from left) and wife Pilar (middle row, fifth from left) stand with four generations of the Wayne family. John Wayne's rise from relative poverty to global fame stands as a success story of the American dream.

BACKCOUNTRY PORK ROAST

Few things bring a smile to a man's face faster than the smell of a roast like this one filling the house.

SERVES 4–6

SUPPLIES

- 2 Tbsp. extra-virgin olive oil
- 1 (2-lb.) pork roast, trimmed and tied
- Kosher salt and pepper, to taste
- 1 medium white or yellow onion, peeled and sliced
- 1 medium apple, cored and sliced
- 1 medium pear, cored and sliced
- 12 oz. apple cider

DIRECTIONS

In a Dutch oven or oven-proof covered pan, heat the oil over medium. Season the pork on all sides generously with salt and pepper. Brown the pork on all sides, about 4 minutes per side. Remove the pork from the pan and set aside. Add the onion, apple and pear to the pan. Season with a large pinch of salt and pepper. Cook until soft and beginning to brown, about 8 minutes.

Pour in the cider, scraping the pan to release any of the brown bits at the bottom of the pan. Add the pork back into the pan. Cover and bake in the oven until the pork registers 145 degrees F on an instant read thermometer, about 40 minutes. Remove the pork from the pan, place it on a cutting board and tent with foil. Let sit for 10 minutes. Puree the cider mixture in a blender. Pour back into the pan and bring to a boil. Season to taste with salt and pepper. Slice the pork and serve with the gravy on the side.

DID YOU KNOW?
Duke loved hunting, especially near the White Mountains of Arizona, where he would stop at lodges for a game of cards and to converse with the locals.

DUKE'S BURGERS

Like John Wayne, these burgers are quintessentially American and guaranteed to be a favorite with your family.

SERVES 6

SUPPLIES

1½ lb. ground chuck

½ lb. ground sirloin

1 tsp. kosher salt

¾ tsp. black pepper

3 Tbsp. melted butter or extra-virgin olive oil

6 hamburger buns

DIRECTIONS

Preheat the grill to medium-high.

Combine the ground chuck, sirloin, salt and pepper. Gently mix with your hands, being careful not to over-mix. Divide the meat into 6 equal portions. Shape into flat, uniform patties. Using your thumb, make an indentation in the center of each patty.

Cook 5 minutes per side for medium burgers. Before taking the burgers off the grill, brush them with melted butter or olive oil.

Toast the buns on the grill if desired and serve with the burgers.

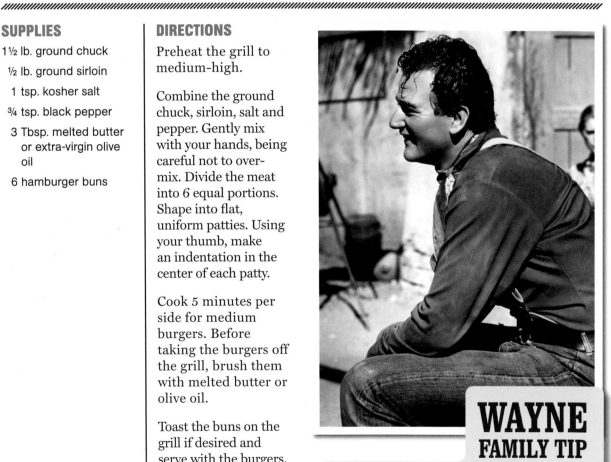

WAYNE FAMILY TIP

You can flavor these burgers any way you wish! Add in garlic powder, soy sauce (if using, skip the salt) or mix in grated cheese for a fun twist.

OLD WESTERN SPICY HONEY RIBS

The sweet and tangy taste of these juicy ribs will remain on your mind long after you've picked the bones clean.

SERVES 4–6

SUPPLIES

- 2 slabs (about 3 lb.) baby back ribs
- Kosher or fine sea salt, to taste
- Pepper, to taste
- 1 cup honey
- ¼ cup tamari or soy sauce
- ¼ cup Dijon mustard
- 5 Tbsp. Sriracha sauce
- 2 tsp. dry ginger
- 2 limes, juiced

DIRECTIONS

Preheat oven to 325 degrees F.

Flip the ribs bone side up and insert a dinner knife just under the white membrane that covers the meat and bones. Gently peel the membrane off. Season the ribs on all sides generously with salt and pepper.

Wrap each rack of ribs with heavy duty foil. Place on a baking sheet and bake for 2 hours 30 minutes to 3 hours or until the meat is tender.

While the ribs are cooking, combine the honey, tamari, mustard, Sriracha, ginger and lime juice in a saucepan. Bring to a boil. Reduce heat and let simmer until the mixture is reduced by half, about 10 minutes.

When the ribs have finished baking, remove from the oven, place the top rack about 8 inches from the broiler, and preheat the broiler to high.

Line 1–2 baking sheets with foil. Unwrap the ribs and place the ribs bone side down on the baking sheets. Brush with the sauce and broil 3 minutes. Brush with more sauce and broil another 2 to 3 minutes.

Serve the ribs with any extra sauce on the side.

DID YOU KNOW?

Rio Lobo (1970) was the last collaboration between Duke and famed director Howard Hawks, who previously worked with John Wayne on *Red River* (1948), *Rio Bravo* (1959), *Hatari!* (1962) and *El Dorado* (1966).

SHREDDED BEEF

The only thing wrong about this dish is that you're not eating it right now.

SERVES 8–10

SUPPLIES

1 (4- to-5 lb.) beef chuck roast

2 cups prepared salsa

DIRECTIONS

Use a 6-quart slow cooker. Place the meat into the slow cooker insert and add the salsa. Cover and cook on low for 8 to 10 hours or on high for about 6 hours. Your meat is finished cooking when it has relaxed and begun to lose shape. If your meat isn't finished after the allotted cooking time, you can "help" by cutting the roast into a few pieces, then continuing to slow cook on high for another hour.

Shred the meat completely using two forks. Cool and store in meal-sized portions in freezer bags or airtight plastic containers. Or eat up now.

WAYNE
FAMILY TIP

If you want more vegetables built into this dish, add one or two sliced onions to the bottom of your slow cooker.

FISH TACOS

These tacos are the perfect companion for a cool breeze and an evening on the water.

SERVES 4

SUPPLIES

- 2 lb. white fish, such as tilapia, cod or halibut
- ½ tsp. kosher salt
- ¼ tsp. black pepper
- ½ cup sour cream
- ½ cup shredded coleslaw mix (shredded cabbage and carrots)
- 2 Tbsp. salsa
- 8 (6-inch) corn tortillas, for serving
- Lime wedges (optional)
- Chopped cilantro (optional)
- Avocado slices (optional)

DIRECTIONS

Use a 4- or 6-quart slow cooker. Cube the fish and toss the cubes with salt and pepper. Place the fish pieces into the center of a length of foil or parchment paper. Fold over the edges and crimp to make a packet. Place the packet into your slow cooker insert.

Cover and cook on high for 2 hours or until the fish flakes easily with a fork. In a mixing bowl, combine the sour cream, coleslaw mix and salsa. Spoon this sauce on top of the fish and serve in warmed corn tortillas with desired garnishes.

WAYNE
FAMILY TIP

Short on time? You can grill or pan-fry the fish instead.

Duke and friend and fellow actor Ward Bond on set on the film *The Wings of Eagles* (1957). Bond and Duke were teammates on the University of Southern California's football team.

HOLIDAY HONEY HAM

This main course will have you lamenting that Christmas only comes once a year. There's always New Year's Day.

SERVES 8

SUPPLIES

- 1 (6- to 7-lb.) bone-in spiral-cut ham
- ¼ cup honey
- ¼ cup spicy brown mustard
- ¼ tsp. ground ginger
- ¼ tsp. ground cloves
- ¼ tsp. ground cinnamon
- 1 orange, juiced
- 1 lemon, juiced
- 1 lime, juiced
- 1 cup ginger ale

DIRECTIONS

Use a 6-quart slow cooker. Unwrap the ham. If there is a flavor packet included, discard it. Place the ham into the slow cooker insert (flat side down).

In a small bowl, combine the honey, mustard, ginger, cloves and cinnamon. Smear this paste on top of the ham, allowing some to drip between the slices. Add all of the citrus juice and a little bit of the pulp to the empty mustard sauce bowl. Stir to combine. Pour this into the slow cooker.

Add the ginger ale. Cover and cook on low for 6 hours or on high for about 3 hours.

DID YOU KNOW?
Duke loved Christmas and would spend hours picking out gifts for his loved ones!

GLAZED SALMON WITH EDAMAME RICE

There's nothing fishy going on here. Just a darn good dish that's light but filling.

SERVES 4

SUPPLIES

Salmon

- ¼ cup soy sauce
- ¼ cup firmly packed brown sugar
- 1 tsp. sesame oil
- 4 (4-oz.) salmon fillets, skin removed
- 1 Tbsp. rice wine vinegar
- 2 scallions, finely sliced on the diagonal
- 1 tsp. sesame seeds

Rice

- 2 cups water
- ½ tsp. kosher salt
- 2 tsp. soy sauce
- 2 Tbsp. rice wine vinegar
- 2 tsp. sesame oil
- ½ tsp. sugar
- 1 cup brown rice
- 1 (2.25-oz.) bag freeze dried soybeans

DIRECTIONS

Salmon

In a shallow baking dish, combine the soy sauce, brown sugar and sesame oil. Add the salmon fillets and let marinate for 3 minutes. Flip and let marinate on the other side.

Heat a large skillet over medium-high. Add the salmon fillets and cook for 2 minutes. Flip the salmon over and cook for another 2 to 4 minutes, depending on how done you like your salmon. Remove from pan and pour the marinade into the hot skillet. Add the rice vinegar and cook, stirring until the sauce reduces slightly, about 2 minutes. Pour the sauce over the salmon, garnish with the scallions and sesame seeds. Serve immediately.

Rice

Combine the water, salt, soy sauce, vinegar, sesame oil, sugar, rice and soy beans in a saucepan, stir to combine and bring to a boil. Cover the pan, reduce to a simmer and let simmer for 20 to 25 minutes or until all the water has evaporated. Fluff with a fork, cover and let sit for 5 minutes.

WAYNE FAMILY TIP

When the salmon flakes easily with a fork, that's a good sign the fish is done.

Duke holds daughter Aissa with wife Pilar (far right) and friends while on vacation. Favorite destinations of the Wayne family included Catalina Island and Mexico.

STANDING RIB ROAST

It takes some time to get this roast ready—but you'll realize it was more than worth the wait the second you take that first bite.

SERVES 10–12

SUPPLIES

1 (9- to 10-lb.) rib roast

Kosher salt
and pepper, for
seasoning

DIRECTIONS

Allow roast to come to room temperature, about 1 hour.

Preheat oven to 450 degrees F.

Place the roast in a heavy metal roasting pan, fat side up, and season generously with salt and pepper. Roast for 30 minutes, reduce the oven temperature to 350 degrees F and roast for another 1 hour 30 minutes to 1 hour 45 minutes, or until an instant read thermometer inserted deep into the center reaches 115 degrees F for rare. Begin checking the internal temperature after 1 hour so as not to overcook the roast. Let stand for 20 minutes (internal temperature should raise to 125 degrees F) before carving and serving.

DID YOU KNOW?

As a youngster growing up in California, Duke would help his father with chores around the farm, waking up early in the morning to pitch in.

LONE STAR SKILLET MAC & CHEESE

Nobody told this mac & cheese that it was just a side dish. Feel free to serve it as the centerpiece of your evening meal or a complement to your favorite main course.

SERVES 6

SUPPLIES

- 4 cups pasta (short cut such as spirals or bow ties)
- 1 tsp. kosher salt to taste, plus more
- 3 cups water
- 1 (12-oz.) can evaporated milk
- 1 (10-oz.) can diced tomatoes and green chilies, undrained
- 1 cup shredded mozzarella cheese
- Pepper, to taste

DIRECTIONS

Combine the pasta, 1 tsp. salt and water in a large skillet. Bring to a boil over high heat. Cook, stirring occasionally, until almost all of the water is gone and the pasta is tender.

Add the evaporated milk and tomatoes. Bring to a boil. Reduce heat to medium and cook until the mixture thickens, about 5 minutes. Add the cheese and cook, stirring, until the cheese is melted. Add additional salt and pepper to taste.

WAYNE FAMILY TIP

Don't be shy about putting your own mark on this recipe. Adding spices such as thyme, oregano, garlic powder and more can result in a delicious surprise.

John Wayne on the set of *Donovan's Reef* (1963) with his friend and mentor, director John Ford. The film was the last time the two legends worked together on a film.

TRAIL HAND BEEF AND BEAN SANDWICHES

You work hard all day. You shouldn't have to work hard on dinner too. These sandwiches are the ones you deserve.

SERVES 6–8

SUPPLIES

- 1 (3-lb.) beef chuck roast
- 1 medium yellow onion, thinly sliced
- 6 garlic cloves, minced
- 1 (15-oz.) can pinto beans, drained and rinsed
- ⅓ cup soy sauce
- ¼ cup dark molasses
- ½ cup barbecue sauce
- ½ tsp. liquid smoke

For serving

- Hoagie rolls
- Sliced cheese
- Pickled jalapeño slices

DIRECTIONS

Use a 6-quart slow cooker. Place the roast into your cooker insert and add the onion rings (separate the rings a bit with your fingers). Add the garlic, beans, soy sauce, molasses, barbecue sauce and liquid smoke. Use kitchen tongs to flip the roast over a few times to help distribute the ingredients.

Cover and cook on low for 10 to 12 hours. Shred the meat completely with 2 large forks before serving in toasted hoagie rolls with cheese and jalapeño slices.

WAYNE
FAMILY TIP

For a milder sandwich, switch out the pickled jalapeño slices with cherry peppers.

CHICKEN THIGHS WITH CHIMICHURRI SAUCE

Duke liked things a bit on the spicy side. This chicken dish would have fit the bill nicely.

SERVES 6

SUPPLIES

- 10 garlic cloves, peeled and roughly chopped
- 2 bunches flat leaf parsley
- ½ cup sherry vinegar or white balsamic vinegar
- 2 tsp. dried oregano
- 1 tsp. red pepper flakes
- 1½ cups plus 3 Tbsp. extra-virgin olive oil, divided
- 12 boneless, skinless chicken thighs
- Kosher salt and pepper, to taste

DIRECTIONS

Put the garlic cloves and parsley in a food processor and pulse until finely chopped. Add the vinegar, oregano and red pepper flakes and process until combined. With the machine running, slowly drizzle in 1 ½ cups olive oil.

In a large plastic food storage bag, combine 6 Tbsp. of the sauce with the remaining 3 Tbsp. of olive oil. Add the chicken thighs and marinate at room temperature for 30 minutes or refrigerate for up to 12 hours. Reserve the rest of the sauce for serving. Remove the thighs from the marinade, pat dry and season with salt and pepper.

Heat a gas or charcoal grill to medium-high. Place the thighs over direct heat, close the barbecue lid and grill for 4 to 6 minutes per side or until the juices from the thickest part of the thigh run clear.

To serve, spoon some of the sauce over the thighs and serve the rest on the side.

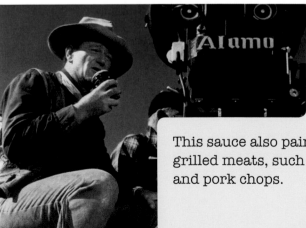

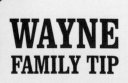

WAYNE FAMILY TIP

This sauce also pairs well with other grilled meats, such as skirt steak and pork chops.

Duke and his daughters Melinda (left) and Antonia (right) are all smiles in this photo from 1954. Both girls appeared as extras in their father's 1952 film *The Quiet Man*.

BEEF TENDERLOIN WITH HORSERADISH SAUCE

When you get the right flavors together, it's hard to go wrong.

SERVES 10

SUPPLIES

- 1 (4-lb.) fully trimmed and tied beef tenderloin
- 4 Tbsp. extra-virgin olive oil
- 3 Tbsp. grainy mustard
- 2 garlic cloves, minced or grated
- 2 Tbsp. minced fresh rosemary
- 2 Tbsp. minced fresh thyme leaves
- 1 Tbsp. kosher salt
- 1½ tsp. pepper
- 1½ cups sour cream
- 4 Tbsp. prepared horseradish

DIRECTIONS

Dry the meat well with paper towels. Combine the oil, mustard, garlic, rosemary, thyme, salt and pepper to form a paste and spread liberally over the beef. Cover with plastic wrap and let sit at room temperature for 30 to 60 minutes. Preheat the oven to 500 degrees F.

Place the beef on a foil-lined, rimmed baking sheet and roast for 30 minutes or until an instant read thermometer inserted into the center reaches 120 degrees F for medium rare. Remove from the oven, tent with foil and let sit for 30 minutes.

Combine the sour cream and horseradish and serve with the tenderloin.

DID YOU KNOW?

Although Duke passed away more than 35 years ago, he remains one of America's favorite actors, according to the annual Harris Poll.

SLOW COOKER CHICKEN

Put this recipe together in the morning before work and come home to find a mouth-watering dinner waiting for the eatin'.

SERVES 6

SUPPLIES

- 1 large onion, peeled and sliced into thin rings
- 3-4 lb. bone-in chicken pieces
- 1 Tbsp. extra-virgin olive oil
- 2 tsp. kosher salt
- 2 tsp. paprika
- 1 tsp. black pepper
- 20-40 garlic cloves, peeled, but intact

DIRECTIONS

Use a 6-quart or larger slow cooker. Separate the onion rings with your fingers and place them into the bottom of the stoneware insert. In a large mixing bowl, toss the chicken pieces with the olive oil, salt, paprika, pepper and all of the garlic cloves. Pour into the slow cooker on top of the onions. Do not add water.

Cover and cook on low for 6 to 8 hours, or on high for 4 to 6 hours. The longer you cook chicken on the bone, the more tender it will be, although it might fall completely off the bone. If you use drumsticks, the ones on the side will brown and may stick to the sides of the slow cooker, burning a bit. If this bothers you, you can rearrange them with tongs an hour before serving.

Serve with a green salad and a side of roasted sweet potatoes, if desired.

DID YOU KNOW?
Despite being a lifelong Republican, John Wayne wrote a letter to new President Jimmy Carter, congratulating him on his electoral victory, despite being a member of the "loyal opposition."

John Wayne and son Ethan on the set of *The Sons of Katie Elder* (1965). Besides its exciting action, the movie also contains great performances by Dean Martin and a young Dennis Hopper.

BLACK BEAN TOSTADAS

While our Spanish dictionaries insist "tostada" translates to "toasted," we're pretty sure it should mean "an unbelievably easy and delicious meal."

SERVES 6

SUPPLIES

Grapeseed or vegetable oil, for frying

12 corn tortillas

Refried black beans, fresh or canned

½ head iceburg lettuce, thinly sliced

Kosher salt and pepper, to taste

Pico de gallo (optional)

8 oz. queso fresco or Monterey Jack cheese, crumbled or grated (optional)

DIRECTIONS

Preheat oven to 250 degrees F. Line a baking sheet with paper towels.

Pour enough oil in a large skillet to reach ¼-inch. Heat over medium until the oil sizzles but does not smoke. Add 1 tortilla at a time and fry until golden brown, about 30 seconds. Flip and fry the other side until golden brown. Remove to the paper towel-lined baking sheet and keep warm in the oven until all the tortillas are fried.

Heat the refried black beans. Season the lettuce with salt and pepper.

To serve, layer the fried tortillas with the refried black beans, lettuce, some pico de gallo and crumbled cheese.

WAYNE
FAMILY TIP

When you add the tortilla to the skillet, it should sizzle immediately. Otherwise, the oil is not hot enough!

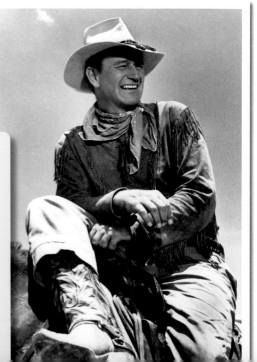

FINGER-LICKIN' FRIED CHICKEN

When you cook this all-American classic to share with the ones you love, everyone's a winner.

SERVES 6–8

SUPPLIES

3-4 lb. cut up chicken pieces

1 qt. buttermilk

3 large eggs

1 tsp. hot sauce

1 cup superfine white flour

⅓ cup cornmeal starch

1 tsp. kosher salt, plus more for seasoning

½ tsp. pepper, plus more for seasoning

1 tsp. garlic powder

1 tsp. paprika

Vegetable oil

DIRECTIONS

Place the chicken pieces in a baking dish and pour on the buttermilk. Cover with plastic wrap and refrigerate for 2 hours or overnight. Remove the chicken from the buttermilk and pat dry with paper towels. Season liberally with salt and pepper.

Whisk the eggs together in a bowl with hot sauce.

In another bowl, whisk together the flour, starch, 1 tsp. salt, ½ tsp. pepper, garlic powder and paprika.

Dip the chicken pieces into the egg mixture then shake off the excess egg and coat well with the flour mixture. Push the flour into the chicken to coat well. Place on a plate and, once all the chicken is coated, let sit for 5 minutes. Coat the chicken in the flour mixture again.

Line a baking sheet with paper towels and place a wire cooling rack on top. Preheat oven to 200 degrees F.

Fill a large, deep frying pan or Dutch oven halfway with oil. Insert a frying or candy thermometer. Heat oil to 380 degrees F. Once the oil is to temperature, carefully lower the chicken into the hot oil, do not crowd the pan. Let cook for 4 minutes and flip over. Cook for 4 more minutes. You may have to adjust the temperature to keep the oil at 380 degrees F.

Remove the cooked chicken and place on the cooling rack, sprinkle with a little salt. Place in oven to keep warm while finishing up the rest of the chicken. Let the oil come back up to temperature and repeat with remaining chicken.

WAYNE FAMILY TIP

A cast-iron skillet ensures even heat distribution during frying and is part of any respectable kitchen.

PACIFIC COAST GRILLED SWORDFISH

Nothing satisfied John Wayne more than reeling in a trophy fish. Except for sharing his bounty with friends and family for dinner.

SERVES 4

SUPPLIES

4-6 oz. swordfish fillets

¼ cup plus 2 Tbsp. orange sauce, divided

2 large oranges, peeled

¼ cup olive oil

1 tsp. kosher or fine sea salt

½ tsp. pepper

1 large fennel bulb, sliced

DIRECTIONS

Place the swordfish fillets in a large plastic storage bag. Add ¼ cup orange sauce and gently shake to coat the fillets with sauce. Marinate in the refrigerator for 30 minutes. Heat grill to medium-high (450 degrees F).

Cut the oranges into segments over a plate or bowl to catch the juice. Measure 1 Tbsp. of orange juice and combine with 2 Tbsp. orange sauce, olive oil, salt and pepper in a medium mixing bowl. Add the sliced fennel and toss gently to combine. Cover and refrigerate until serving time.

Remove swordfish from marinade and discard marinade. Brush grates of the grill with some oil. Grill for 8 minutes with the lid closed, turning once.

Placc the orange and fennel salad on plates and top with the swordfish fillets and serve.

DID YOU KNOW?

Fishing was one of John Wayne's favorite ways to pass the time, and he sailed his boat the *Wild Goose* to many beloved fishing spots up and down America's Pacific Coast.

PULLED CHICKEN WITH COLESLAW

This recipe is perfect for your next cookout, get together or anytime you just want something tasty.

SERVES 8

SUPPLIES

- 3½-4 lb. chicken parts, skin on, bone in
- 4 cups chicken stock or water
- 1 (10-oz.) jar maraschino cherries without stems
- 1 cup ketchup
- ¾ cup pineapple juice
- 1 Tbsp. Worcestershire sauce
- 1 Tbsp. dried garlic
- 1 Tbsp. dried onion
- 1-3 tsp. chipotle chili powder
- ½ cup sour cream
- ½ cup mayonnaise
- 2 tsp. sugar
- 2 limes, juiced
- 1 (14- to 16-oz.) bag coleslaw
- 4 green onions, thinly sliced
- ½ cup fresh cilantro, chopped
- Kosher salt and pepper, to taste
- 8 hamburger buns, toasted or warmed

DIRECTIONS

Place the chicken in a saucepan or Dutch oven with the chicken stock or water. Bring to a boil, cover the pot, reduce heat to a simmer and cook until the chicken is cooked through, about 20 to 25 minutes. Remove the chicken from the liquid, let cool enough to handle then remove the skin and bones and shred.

Puree the maraschino cherries along with their liquid in a blender. Pour into a large saucepan and add the ketchup, pineapple juice, Worcestershire sauce, garlic, onion and chipotle chili powder. Stir to combine. Bring to a boil, reduce heat and simmer, uncovered, until thickened to the consistency of barbecue sauce, about 30 minutes. Add the shredded chicken to the sauce, stirring to combine.

In a large mixing bowl, combine the sour cream, mayonnaise, sugar and lime juice, whisking until smooth. Add the coleslaw, green onions and cilantro. Toss to combine. Season to taste with salt and pepper.

Place some chicken on the bottom half of a hamburger bun, top with coleslaw and the top half of the bun.

WAYNE
FAMILY TIP

When cooking the chicken, add more water or chicken stock if it looks like it is cooking through the liquid.

STEAK SALAD

There are plenty of ways to make a salad delicious. Our favorite method? Add steak.

SERVES 6

SUPPLIES

1½ lb. flank steak

   Kosher salt and pepper, for seasoning

1 cup chimichurri dressing, divided

12 oz. small fresh mozzarella balls, halved

1 pint grape tomatoes, halved

½ red onion, very thinly sliced

½ cup chopped flat leaf parsley

DIRECTIONS

Season the steak generously with salt and pepper. Place in a large food storage bag and add ½ cup dressing. Let marinate at room temperature for 10 to 30 minutes (or refrigerate for up to 8 hours). Remove the steak from the marinade and discard the marinade.

Heat a grill or grill pan to medium-high. Cook the steak 5 minutes per side. Let sit for 10 minutes.

Toss the mozzarella cheese, tomatoes, red onion slices and parsley with ¼ cup dressing. Arrange on a platter. Slice the steak and lay on top of the salad. Drizzle the steak with the remaining ¼ cup dressing.

DID YOU KNOW?

Duke owned a cattle ranch in Arizona, the 26 Bar Ranch, where he and ranch manager Louis Johnson would raise Hereford cattle.

Sidekicks

//

John Wayne always kept a reliable posse of characters around to help him out of a jam. In the same way, these side dishes will perfectly round out any meal you put together.

Quick-Draw Corn Pudding

South-of-the-Border Mexican Rice

Western Green Beans

Roasted Potatoes

Tart Brussels Sprouts

Grilled Shrimp Skewers

Western Baked Beans

Heartland Creamed Corn

Mexican Sweet Potato Salad

Katie McLintock's Spicy Asparagus

Monument Valley Mac and Cheese Meatballs

Zucchini Gratin

Candied Sweet Potatoes

QUICK-DRAW CORN PUDDING

The peppers included in this side dish make sure the flavor explodes in your mouth with every bite.

SERVES 8

SUPPLIES

- 2 cups fresh or frozen corn kernels (thawed if frozen)
- 1 medium red bell pepper, seeded and diced
- 1 small jalapeño pepper, veins and seeds discarded, finely diced
- 1 medium white onion, diced
- 2 Tbsp. all-purpose flour
- 1 tsp. dry mustard
- 1 tsp. kosher salt
- ½ tsp. pepper
- 2 large eggs, lightly beaten
- 1½ cups milk

DIRECTIONS

Preheat oven to 350 degrees F. Spray a 2-quart baking dish with nonstick cooking spray.

In a mixing bowl, combine the corn, peppers, onion, flour, dry mustard, salt and pepper. In another mixing bowl, whisk together the eggs and milk. Add the eggs and milk to the corn mixture and mix well. Pour into the prepared baking dish and bake for 45 minutes or until set.

Can be served warm or at room temperature.

WAYNE FAMILY TIP

To make this recipe a little more decadent, add ½ cup of your favorite shredded cheese. Cheddar or pepper jack both work well.

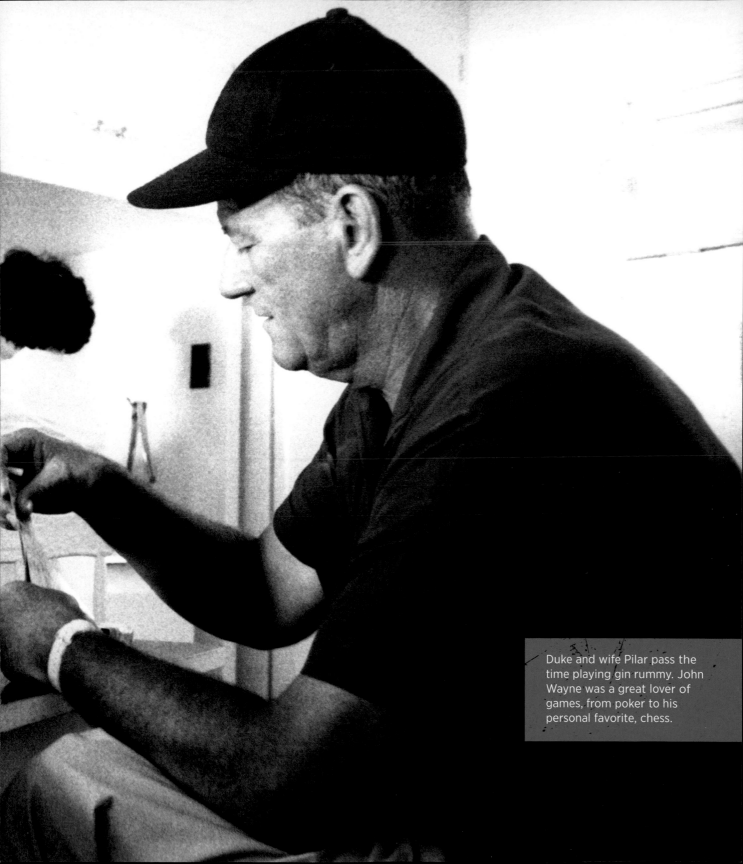

Duke and wife Pilar pass the time playing gin rummy. John Wayne was a great lover of games, from poker to his personal favorite, chess.

SOUTH-OF-THE-BORDER MEXICAN RICE

The perfect pairing with just about anything, this side dish works particularly well with spicier Latin cuisine.

SERVES 6

SUPPLIES

- 2 Tbsp. olive oil
- ½ cup finely chopped onions
- 1 cup risotto rice
- 1 (15-oz.) can of chopped tomatoes
- ½ tsp. ground cumin
- 1 clove garlic
- 1 jalapeño pepper, finely chopped (optional)
- 1 cup chicken stock

DIRECTIONS

Heat a large skillet over medium-high. Add olive oil and chopped onions. Cook until onions are soft but not browned, about 3 minutes. Add the rice and cook, stirring, for 2 more minutes until the rice starts to look translucent. Put onion/rice mixture into a microwave-safe casserole dish with a lid. Put chopped tomatoes with their juice, ground cumin, garlic and jalapeño (if using) into a blender and blend until smooth. Add enough chicken stock to make 3 cups of liquid and blend.

Add the tomato/chicken stock mixture to the rice, stir, cover with the lid, and microwave on high for about 18 to 20 minutes. Stir 3 times while cooking. Remove from microwave, stir, replace lid and let stand 5 minutes. If not using the microwave, then add the tomato/chicken stock mixture to the rice in the skillet in 1-cup increments, stirring after each addition of liquid until fully absorbed.

DID YOU KNOW?

John Wayne knew the importance of enjoying a good meal. Once asked by *Variety* how he avoided overeating at lunch, he responded "I don't avoid overeating."

WESTERN GREEN BEANS

There's nothing complicated about this dish, but you don't have to tell anybody.

SERVES 12

SUPPLIES

- 6 large onions, peeled, each cut through vertically through root end into 12 or 14 wedges
- 6 Tbsp. unsalted butter, divided
- Salt and pepper, for seasoning
- 2 cups canned chicken broth
- 3 Tbsp. sugar
- 2 Tbsp. balsamic vinegar
- 3 lb. slender green beans, ends trimmed

DIRECTIONS

Preheat oven to 450 degrees F. Spray 2 heavy baking sheets with nonstick spray. Arrange onion wedges in a single layer on the baking sheets and dot with 4 Tbsp. of butter. Season with salt and pepper.

Bake until onions are dark brown stirring once or twice, about 40 minutes. While onions are baking, boil broth in a large, heavy skillet over high heat until reduced to about ½ cup, about 6 to 8 minutes. Add sugar and vinegar and cook, stirring, until sugar dissolves and the mixture comes to a boil. Add the onions to the sauce and reduce heat to medium-low. Simmer until the liquid is reduced and syrupy, about 5 minutes. Season with salt and pepper. Can be prepared 1 day ahead. Cover and refrigerate. Reheat over low heat or in microwave.

Cook green beans in a large pot of boiling salted water until crisp tender, about 5 minutes. Drain well. Return to same pot, add remaining 2 Tbsp. of butter and toss to coat. If making ahead, cook beans for about 4 minutes, drain and rinse with cold water to stop the cooking. Wrap in paper towels, then in cling-wrap and refrigerate until just before serving time. Heat 2 Tbsp. of butter in a large skillet or pot, add green beans and re-heat. Serve beans in a large shallow bowl topped with onions.

WAYNE
FAMILY TIP

The best way to make sure the beans retain their fresh, bright green color is to blanch them in a bowl of ice water for a few moments after they're finished boiling.

ROASTED POTATOES

The old trail hands didn't have time to slave over fussy, elaborate recipes. Fortunately, as this standout side dish proves, that doesn't mean they skimped on taste.

SERVES 12

SUPPLIES

3 lb. baby Yukon gold potatoes

6 slices thick-cut bacon

Olive oil

½ tsp. kosher salt

½ tsp. pepper

½ cup fresh Italian parsley, chopped

DIRECTIONS

Preheat oven to 350 degrees F. Scrub potatoes and place in a large saucepan covered with salted water. Bring to a boil and cook for 5 minutes. Drain.

Cut bacon into small pieces and fry over medium heat until the fat has rendered and the bacon bits are crispy. Drain the bacon on paper towels and reserve. Pour the bacon fat into a measuring cup and add enough olive oil to make ½ cup.

Place potatoes in a roasting pan, add the bacon fat mixture, salt and pepper and toss to coat. Bake for 1 hour or until the potatoes are fork tender, stirring once or twice while cooking. Toss potatoes with the reserved bacon bits and parsley and serve.

DID YOU KNOW?
Duke's characters carried a variety of weapons, such as the Winchester 1892 rifle, into their on-screen battles.

TART BRUSSELS SPROUTS

Add a little zip to an old standby to create a vegetable dish they'll be raving about for weeks.

SERVES 12

SUPPLIES

- 3 lb. Brussels sprouts, woody ends cut off, outer leaves removed and discarded, sprouts cut in half lengthwise
- 3 Tbsp. olive oil
- ½ tsp. kosher salt
- ½ tsp. pepper
- 1 cup pomegranate juice
- 3 Tbsp. honey
- 1 Tbsp. fresh lemon juice
- Seeds from 1 pomegranate

DIRECTIONS

Preheat oven to 400 degrees F. Toss Brussels sprouts with the olive oil, salt and pepper. Place on a baking sheet in a single layer and cook for 25 minutes or until tender and starting to brown.

In a saucepan, combine the pomegranate juice, honey and lemon juice and bring to a boil. Cook until it begins to thicken slightly, about 5 minutes. Let cool (mixture will thicken a bit more as it cools).

Toss Brussels sprouts with the syrup and pomegranate seeds. Serve warm.

WAYNE FAMILY TIP

To avoid mushy sprouts, make sure not to crowd the pan when roasting.

GRILLED SHRIMP SKEWERS

While this recipe of grilled goodness can take center stage as a main dish,
one or two skewers can also brighten up any meal.

SERVES 6

SUPPLIES

6 skewers

6 Tbsp. Asian
barbecue sauce

3 Tbsp. butter, melted

1½ lb. large shrimp,
peeled, deveined,
tail on

Vegetable oil

DIRECTIONS

If using wooden skewers, soak in water for 30 minutes.

Combine the Asian barbecue sauce and melted butter and pour into a
large food storage bag. Add the shrimp, close the bag and flip several
times to coat the shrimp. Marinate in the refrigerator for 10 minutes.

Thread 2 to 3 shrimp on each skewer. Discard any remaining marinade.

Heat grill to medium-high, brush the grill grates with oil and grill the
skewers for 2 minutes per side.

— DID YOU KNOW?

Duke would sail with
friends and family to
destinations as varied as
the waters around Mexico
to the Pacific Northwest.

WESTERN BAKED BEANS

Make a great meal even better by adding this hearty side to the menu.

SERVES 8

SUPPLIES

- 6 slices applewood-smoked bacon, diced
- 1 medium yellow onion, peeled and diced
- 4 garlic cloves, minced
- 4 (15-oz.) cans white beans, drained and rinsed
- 1 cup root beer
- 1 Tbsp. apple cider vinegar
- 2 Tbsp. molasses
- 2 Tbsp. tomato paste
- 2 Tbsp. Dijon mustard
- 1 tsp. chili powder
- 1 tsp. kosher salt
- ½ tsp. pepper

DIRECTIONS

In a large skillet over medium heat, cook the bacon, onion and garlic, stirring, until the bacon is cooked. Drain off any accumulated fat and transfer the bacon mixture into a 4-quart slow cooker. Add the beans and root beer.

In a small bowl, combine the vinegar, molasses, tomato paste, mustard, chili powder, salt and pepper. Stir this sauce into the beans. Cover and cook on low for 8 hours.

WAYNE
FAMILY TIP

Don't use diet root beer! You want real sugar to sweeten these beans.

HEARTLAND CREAMED CORN

You don't have to wait until summer to enjoy this delicious, creamy side dish.

SERVES 8

SUPPLIES

- 2 cups fresh or frozen white corn
- 1 (15-oz.) can corn niblets, liquid reserved
- 1 Tbsp. salted butter
- 1 Tbsp. cream cheese, softened
- 2 Tbsp. all-purpose flour
- 3 Tbsp. milk
- ¼ tsp. pepper

DIRECTIONS

Use a 4-quart slow cooker. Pour the frozen corn and the niblets from the canned corn into your slow cooker. Retain the liquid from the canned corn.

In a small saucepan on the stovetop, melt the butter and cream cheese over low heat. Slowly add the flour. Whisk until the flour is fully incorporated and remove from heat. Stir in the milk, juice from the canned corn and pepper. Pour this mixture evenly over the top of the corn in the slow cooker. Stir to combine. Cover and cook on low for 4 to 6 hours or on high for about 3 hours.

DID YOU KNOW?

Duke recorded a spoken-word album called *America, Why I Love Her*, which was first released in 1972.

John Wayne and his wife Pilar share a tender moment on a plane. The two often vacationed together in Hawaii, the place where they tied the knot.

MEXICAN SWEET POTATO SALAD

You may as well double this recipe at the outset—seconds, and even thirds, will be demanded.

SERVES 6

SUPPLIES

- 4 medium sweet potatoes, peeled and cut into 1-inch cubes
- 1 red onion, cut into 1-inch pieces
- 2 Tbsp. plus ¼ cup olive oil, divided
- 1 tsp. kosher salt, plus more to taste
- ½ tsp. pepper, plus more to taste
- 1 (15-oz.) can black beans, drained and rinsed
- 1 red bell pepper, seeded and chopped
- ½ cup roughly chopped fresh cilantro
- 1 jalapeño pepper, seeded, deveined and roughly chopped
- 1 garlic clove, roughly chopped
- ¼ cup orange sauce

DIRECTIONS

Preheat oven to 400 degrees F. Place the sweet potatoes and onions on a rimmed baking sheet. Drizzle with 2 Tbsp. olive oil, add 1 tsp. salt, ½ tsp. pepper and toss to coat. Roast, turning once or twice, for 30 minutes or until the sweet potatoes are tender and starting to brown. Remove from oven and let cool.

In a large bowl, combine the cooled sweet potatoes and onions with the black beans, red pepper and cilantro.

Place the jalapeño and garlic in the blender and pulse several times to finely chop. Add the orange sauce and ¼ cup olive oil and blend until smooth. Taste and add salt and pepper, if desired. Pour the dressing over the vegetables and toss to coat. Serve at room temperature or cold.

WAYNE
FAMILY TIP

Squeeze a little fresh lime over this salad when you serve it to brighten the flavors.

KATIE McLINTOCK'S SPICY ASPARAGUS

A hot and delicious veggie recipe as fiery as the character it's named after.

SERVES 6

SUPPLIES

- 2 large shallots
- Vegetable oil
- Kosher salt
- 2 lb. asparagus
- 4 Tbsp. peanut butter
- 4 Tbsp. tamari or soy sauce
- 2 Tbsp. honey
- 1 Tbsp. rice vinegar
- 1 Tbsp. chili garlic sauce
- 2 tsp. toasted sesame oil

DIRECTIONS

Line a plate with paper towels. Slice the shallots thinly then separate into rings. Heat about ¼ of an inch of oil in a medium skillet over high until hot. Add the shallot rings and cook, stirring frequently, until browned, about 6 minutes. With a slotted spoon, remove the shallots and place on the paper towels to drain. Sprinkle with salt.

With a vegetable peeler, peel the asparagus. Cut off the woody end. Place in a large skillet and cover with water. Bring to a boil and cook for 2 to 3 minutes or until crisp tender. Remove the asparagus from the skillet and pour out the water.

To the same skillet, add the peanut butter, tamari, honey, vinegar, chili garlic sauce and sesame oil. Heat, stirring, until smooth and heated through. If the sauce is too thick, add a little water, about 1 Tbsp. at a time, until thinned out. You want the sauce to still be thick, but runny.

Add the asparagus to the sauce and gently toss to coat. Place the asparagus on a serving platter and top with the fried shallots.

DID YOU KNOW?

Maureen O'Hara, the late, great actress who played Katie in *McLintock!*, was a personal friend of Duke's off the set as well.

MONUMENT VALLEY MAC AND CHEESE MEATBALLS

You'd better bookmark this page—this recipe is so delicious, you'll have to cook it time and again.

MAKES 24 MEATBALLS

SUPPLIES

- 1 (5-oz.) package mac and cheese
- 1½ lb. lean ground beef or turkey
- 1 small onion, grated
- 1 small carrot, grated
- 1 cup breadcrumbs
- 1 tsp. kosher salt
- ½ tsp. pepper

DIRECTIONS

Preheat oven to 425 degrees F. Line two baking sheets with parchment paper.

Prepare the mac and cheese according to the package directions, omitting the additional milk and butter. Let cool for 10 minutes.

Combine the ground beef with the grated onion and carrot, bread crumbs, salt and pepper. Add in the prepared mac and cheese. Using about ¼ cup per meatball, roll into balls. Place on prepared baking sheets, spray with nonstick cooking spray and bake for 20 minutes or until they are browned. The meatballs will feel soft; they firm up a little as they cool. Let cool for 5 minutes and serve.

DID YOU KNOW?
John Wayne made some of his most memorable films with director John Ford, inlcuding *The Searchers* (1956), left, often shooting in Monument Valley, located on the Arizona-Utah border.

ZUCCHINI GRATIN

Venture off the beaten path to discover this delicious, cheese-smothered side dish that's sure to be a hit.

SERVES 6–8

SUPPLIES

- 1 cup milk
- 1 Tbsp. cornstarch
- 6 Tbsp. olive oil, divided
- 3 medium white or yellow onions, cut in half and thinly sliced
- 2 tsp. kosher or fine sea salt
- 1 tsp. pepper
- ¼ tsp. freshly grated nutmeg
- 4 medium zucchini
- ¼ cup sundried tomatoes packed in oil, dried and finely chopped
- ½ cup minced fresh basil leaves
- ¾ cup breadcrumbs
- ¼ cup shredded cheese

DIRECTIONS

Preheat oven to 400 degrees F.

Mix ¼ cup milk with the cornstarch and set aside.

Heat 4 Tbsp. of olive oil in a large skillet over low heat. Add the onions and salt and cook until the onions are very tender but not brown, about 20 minutes. Cut the zucchini in half lengthwise, then slice about ¼-inch thick. Add the pepper, nutmeg, zucchini, sundried tomatoes and remaining ¾ cup of milk to the onions, raise the heat to medium, cover the pan and cook for 10 minutes or until the zucchini is fork tender.

Remove the cover, raise the heat to high, bring the mixture to a boil and stir in the milk starch mixture. Cook the mixture, stirring until the mixture thickens, about 1 minute. Remove from the heat and stir in the basil.

Combine the breadcrumbs with the cheese. Put the zucchini mixture into a 9- by 12-inch (or similar sized) baking dish, top with the breadcrumb mixture and drizzle the top with the remaining 2 Tbsp. of olive oil. Bake for 20 minutes or until bubbly and browned.

WAYNE FAMILY TIP

This recipe is the perfect way to use any zucchinis you have leftover that may be a little too soft to put in a salad.

CANDIED SWEET POTATOES

This dish is so tasty folks'll think you're serving dessert alongside their dinner.

SERVES 8

SUPPLIES

1 Tbsp. butter

7-8 sweet potatoes, peeled and sliced ½-inch thick

½ cup orange juice

½ cup firmly packed brown sugar

2 tsp. vanilla extract

1 tsp. ground cinnamon

¼ tsp. kosher salt

½-1 cup mini marshmallows

DIRECTIONS

Use a 4-quart slow cooker. Rub the butter onto the inside of your slow cooker. Layer in the sweet potato slices. In a small mixing bowl, combine the orange juice, brown sugar, vanilla, cinnamon and salt. Pour this mixture evenly over the top of the sweet potatoes.

Cover and cook on low for 6 to 7 hours or on high for 3 to 4 hours. When potatoes are soft, scoop into an oven-safe dish, dot with marshmallows and broil in the oven for 3 to 5 minutes or until marshmallows have just begun to brown.

WAYNE
FAMILY TIP

Be careful not to cook marshmallows for too long or they'll liquify and harden when they start to cool.

Sweet Treats

///

After a hard day's work, you more than
deserve these delicious desserts.

Donovan's Key Lime Pie

Sweet and Salty Chocolate Brownies

Pumpkin Pudding

All-American Apple Pie

Chocolate Chip Cookies

Blueberry Crisp

Pumpkin Walnut Cake

Red, White and Blueberry Cupcakes

Peanut Butter and Chocolate Fudge

Vanilla Wafer Coconut Cake

Patriotic Pavlova

Cranberry Pie

Over-the-Top Chocolate Cake

DONOVAN'S KEY LIME PIE

When the temperature outside starts climbing, this treat is a delicious and refreshing way to keep cool.

SERVES 8

SUPPLIES

- 1 (8-oz.) package cream cheese, at room temperature
- 1 (14-oz.) can sweetened condensed milk
- 3 egg yolks
- ½ cup fresh key lime or lime juice
- 1 pre-made graham cracker crust

DIRECTIONS

Preheat oven to 350 degrees F.

In the bowl of an electric mixer, preferably fitted with a paddle attachment, beat the cream cheese until smooth and creamy. Add the sweetened condensed milk and egg yolks and beat until fully incorporated, scraping down the sides of the bowl as needed. Add the lime juice and beat well.

Pour the mixture into the pie shell and smooth the top with a spatula. Place the pie on a baking sheet and bake for 10 minutes or until the filling begins to set. Let cool completely.

Refrigerate for at least 2 hours or up to 24 hours before serving.

DID YOU KNOW?

Hawaii held many special memories for John Wayne, but none more precious than the small wedding ceremony in Kona on November 1, 1954, which wedded him to Pilar Pallete.

SWEET AND SALTY CHOCOLATE BROWNIES

Chopped peanuts add an extra crunch to an already spectacular recipe.

MAKES 48 BROWNIES

SUPPLIES

- 1¼ cups semisweet chocolate chips
- 1 cup unsalted butter, softened
- 4 large eggs
- 1 cup coconut palm sugar
- 6 Tbsp. unsweetened cocoa powder
- 2 Tbsp. cornstarch
- ½ tsp. kosher salt
- 1 tsp. instant espresso powder
- 2 tsp. pure vanilla extract
- 1½ cups chopped salted, dry-roasted peanuts

DIRECTIONS

Preheat oven to 375 degrees F. Line a 9- by 12-inch baking dish with parchment paper.

Place the chocolate chips and butter into the bowl of a food processor and pulse a few times to roughly combine. Add the eggs, coconut palm sugar, cocoa powder, cornstarch, salt, espresso powder and vanilla, and blitz until combined. The batter will be lumpy. Spread the mixture into the prepared baking dish. Sprinkle the chopped nuts over the top and gently press into the batter. Bake for 20 minutes or until the batter is set and feels slightly firm to the touch. The outer edges will appear drier than the inside. Let cool and then cut into 1 ½-inch squares.

WAYNE
FAMILY TIP

Adding a touch of instant espresso powder to chocolatey desserts mutes the sweetness and gives a more complex flavor to the treat.

John Wayne poses for a photo during a game of chess. An avid player, Duke would often play his costars and family members (who were sometimes one in the same) in between takes while working.

PUMPKIN PUDDING

This creative concoction gives you the tasty filling of pumpkin pie without the hassle of making the crust.

SERVES 8

SUPPLIES

- 1 (15-oz.) can pure pumpkin puree
- 1 (12-oz.) can evaporated milk
- ¾ cup white sugar
- ½ cup biscuit mix
- 2 large eggs
- 2 Tbsp. butter, melted
- 2 tsp. vanilla extract
- 1¼ tsp. ground cinnamon
- ½ tsp. nutmeg
- ¼ tsp. ground cloves
- ⅛ tsp. ground ginger

DIRECTIONS

Use a 4-quart slow cooker sprayed with cooking spray. In a mixing bowl, combine all of the ingredients and whisk until fully blended. Pour the batter into the prepared insert. Cover and cook on high for 3 to 4 hours or on low for about 6 hours. Check your "pie" after 2 hours on high and 3 hours on low. Then check every 30 minutes.

When fully cooked, the pudding will look just like a finished pumpkin pie. The batter will have browned and will crack in a few places. The center will have set enough for you to touch it without getting batter on your finger.

Let it sit in the slow cooker with the lid off until room temperature. Then spoon it into serving dishes and top with whipped cream or serve with vanilla ice cream.

DID YOU KNOW?
Duke didn't only work in front of the camera. In addition to directing, he started producing films in 1947. The first film he produced was *Angel and the Badman*.

ALL-AMERICAN APPLE PIE

A classic recipe enjoyed by Americans for generations, this pie makes a patriotic (and tasty) cap to any meal.

SERVES 8

SUPPLIES

- 2 cups graham-style crumbs, divided
- 4 Tbsp. unsalted butter, melted
- 1 Tbsp. honey
- 4 large apples, peeled, cored and thinly sliced
- ¾ cup brown sugar, divided
- ½ lemon, juiced
- 1 Tbsp. cornstarch
- 1 tsp. ground cinnamon
- ¼ tsp. kosher salt
- 1 tsp. pure vanilla extract
- ½ cup sliced almonds
- 4 Tbsp. unsalted butter, softened

DIRECTIONS

Line a flat baking sheet with foil and place on the lowest rack of the oven (this is to catch any juices that may drip from your pie and keep your oven clean.) Put the other rack in the middle. Preheat oven to 350 degrees F. Spray a 9-inch pie pan with nonstick cooking spray.

Combine 1 ¼ cups graham-style crumbs with the melted butter and honey. Dump the mixture into the prepared pie plate and press firmly on the bottom and up the sides of the pan. Bake for 10 minutes. Leave the oven on.

In a large mixing bowl, combine the sliced apples, ½ cup brown sugar, lemon juice, cornstarch, cinnamon, salt and vanilla and toss to combine. Pour the mixture into the pre-baked pie crust and gently press down on the apples to flatten the top slightly.

Combine the remaining ¼ cup brown sugar with the remaining ¾ cup graham-style crumbs and sliced almonds. Cut the butter into pieces, and with your fingers combine everything until it is clumpy. Spread the mixture over the apples and bake for 80 to 90 minutes or until the apple mixture is hot and bubbly and the crust is browned; after 45 minutes place a piece of foil over the top of the pie to keep it from browning too much.

Let cool and serve.

WAYNE
FAMILY TIP

For extra-flavorful filling, toss the apples with the rest of the pie filling in a plastic bag the night before.

CHOCOLATE CHIP COOKIES

Your family probably thinks they can't be surprised by chocolate chip cookies. Give them a shock with this out-of-this-world recipe.

MAKES 2–4 DOZEN, DEPENDING ON THE SIZE

SUPPLIES

- 1 cup unsalted butter, at room temperature
- 1 cup sugar
- 1 cup light brown sugar
- 2 large eggs, at room temperature
- 1 tsp. pure vanilla extract
- 2 ½ cups oats
- 2 cups all-purpose flour
- ½ tsp. kosher or sea salt
- 1 tsp. baking powder
- 1 tsp. baking soda
- 4 oz. milk chocolate, grated
- 12 oz. semisweet chocolate chips

DIRECTIONS

Preheat oven to 375 degrees F. Line baking sheets with either parchment paper or silicone baking mats.

In the bowl of an electric mixer fitted with a paddle attachment, cream the butter, sugar and brown sugar on medium speed until very light and fluffy, about 5 minutes. Turn mixer to low and add the eggs, one at a time, mixing until each egg is fully mixed in, scraping down the sides of the bowl with each addition. Add the vanilla extract and mix well.

Put the oats in a blender or food processor and grind to a powder. In a large mixing bowl, whisk together the ground oats, flour, salt, baking powder and baking soda.

With the mixer on low, add the flour/oat mixture to the butter mixture gradually and mix until just combined. Add the grated milk chocolate. With a large spatula, scrape the sides and bottom of the mixing bowl and make sure everything is well combined. Fold in the chocolate chips.

Spoon batter onto prepared pans using between 1 and 2 Tbsp. of batter per cookie depending on how large you like them, leaving about 2 inches of space between each cookie.

Bake for 8 to 12 minutes.

Let cookies cool on the pan for 5 minutes and then remove to wire racks to finish cooling.

WAYNE FAMILY TIP

Refrigerating the dough for 30 minutes before baking prevents the cookies from spreading in the oven.

John Wayne with his son Ethan and daughter Marisa enjoy a quiet moment. Despite his celebrity status, Duke didn't put on any airs, driving his children around town in a station wagon.

BLUEBERRY CRISP

This simple dessert can easily be improved with the addition of a single scoop of vanilla ice cream per serving. Or two. Or three!

SERVES 6

SUPPLIES

- 4 cups (four 6-oz. containers) fresh blueberries, rinsed, picked over and drained
- ⅓ cup sugar
- 1 lemon, zested
- 2 tsp. fresh lemon juice
- 1 Tbsp. cornstarch
- ⅓ cup brown sugar, packed
- ⅓ cup flour
- ¾ cup oats
- Pinch kosher salt
- 4 Tbsp. unsalted butter, softened

DIRECTIONS

Preheat oven to 375 degrees F. Grease a 10-inch baking dish or deep dish pie pan.

In a mixing bowl, combine the blueberries, sugar, lemon zest, lemon juice and cornstarch. Toss to coat and pour mixture into prepared baking dish.

In another mixing bowl, combine the brown sugar, flour, oats and salt. Add the butter and work it into the oat mixture with your fingertips until crumbly. Spread over the blueberries and bake for 40 minutes or until the blueberries are bubbly and the topping is golden brown.

DID YOU KNOW?
Duke performed many of his own stunts, particularly in the World War II movie *Back to Bataan* (1945).

PUMPKIN WALNUT CAKE

A wonderfully balanced swirl of spices and flavors, this dish evokes the first day of fall, but is just as tasty in spring.

SERVES 8–10

SUPPLIES

1¾ cups sugar

1 heaping cup pure pumpkin puree (not pumpkin pie filling)

8 large eggs

3¼ cups flour

2 tsp. ground cinnamon

½ tsp. kosher salt

½ tsp. ground cloves

¼ tsp. grated nutmeg

2 tsp. pure vanilla extract

¾ cup chopped walnuts

3 Tbsp. light brown sugar

DIRECTIONS

Preheat oven to 350 degrees F. Line a 10-inch springform pan with parchment paper and spray generously with nonstick cooking spray.

Place the sugar in the food processor and process for 30 seconds. Add the pumpkin, eggs, flour, cinnamon, salt, cloves, nutmeg and vanilla. Process until smooth. Pour into prepared pan and smooth the top.

Combine the walnuts and brown sugar in a small bowl and sprinkle on top of the cake batter. Bake 55 to 65 minutes or until a toothpick inserted into the center comes out clean. Let cool in the pan then remove.

WAYNE
FAMILY TIP

This cake will keep for up to a week, as long as you store it at room temperature. Assuming it lasts that long.

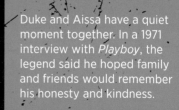

Duke and Aissa have a quiet moment together. In a 1971 interview with *Playboy*, the legend said he hoped family and friends would remember his honesty and kindness.

RED, WHITE AND BLUEBERRY CUPCAKES

Bring a tray of these winners to your next cookout and wait for the compliments to rain down.

MAKES 12 CUPCAKES

SUPPLIES

Cupcakes

1½ cups plus 2 Tbsp. all-purpose flour, divided

1 tsp. baking powder

½ tsp. kosher or fine sea salt

½ cup unsalted butter at room temperature

1 cup sugar

2 large eggs, at room temperature

½ cup milk, at room temperature

1 tsp. pure vanilla extract

¾ cup blueberries, divided

4 Tbsp. maraschino cherry juice

12 maraschino cherries with stems

Red, white and blue sprinkles

Frosting

½ cup unsalted butter, at room temperature

⅛ tsp. kosher or fine sea salt

2½ cups powdered sugar

½ tsp. pure vanilla extract

2 tsp. fresh lemon juice

WAYNE FAMILY TIP

Wait an hour after your cupcakes come out of the oven before frosting. If you frost them while they're still warm, the frosting will melt on top of the cupcakes.

DIRECTIONS

Preheat oven to 350 degrees. Line 12 standard muffin cups with paper liners.

In a large mixing bowl, whisk together 1 ½ cups flour, baking powder and salt.

In the bowl of an electric mixer, cream the butter and sugar together on medium speed for 2 minutes or until light and fluffy. Scrape down the sides of the bowl and add the eggs, one at a time, mixing well and scraping down the sides of the bowl after each addition. Turn the mixer to low, add half the flour mixture, then the milk and finally the remaining flour mixture. Add the vanilla extract and mix well. Scrape the sides and bottom of the bowl with a spatula to make sure all the ingredients are fully combined.

Place ½ cup of blueberries in a small mixing bowl, add 1 Tbsp. of flour and toss the blueberries with the flour. Add ¾ cup of batter and gently fold the blueberries into the batter. Divide the mixture among the prepared muffin cups and smooth down the batter with a small offset spatula, making sure to spread the batter all the way to the sides.

Place ¾ cup of batter in a small bowl, add the remaining Tbsp. of flour and the maraschino cherry juice. Mix well. Gently spoon this batter on top of the blueberry layer. Even out the batter and spread

all the way to the sides. Gently spoon the remaining batter on top of the cherry layer and spread as before. Bake for 20 to 25 minutes or until the tops of the cupcakes start to brown and a toothpick inserted into the center comes out clean. Let the cupcakes cool in the pan for 5 minutes then remove to a wire rack to finish cooling.

While the cupcakes are cooling, make the frosting.

In the bowl of an electric mixer, beat the ½ cup butter with the ⅛ tsp. salt on high speed until creamy. Add the powdered sugar, vanilla and lemon juice and mix, starting on low and increasing the speed until fully combined and fluffy.

Pipe or spread the frosting onto the cooled cupcakes and garnish each cupcake with a maraschino cherry, the remaining blueberries and some sprinkles.

PEANUT BUTTER AND CHOCOLATE FUDGE

PB and chocolate are like Ward Bond and Duke—an always welcome combo that can't miss.

MAKES 20 PIECES OF FUDGE

SUPPLIES

5 Tbsp. unsalted butter, use divided

2 cups light brown sugar

½ cup plus 3 Tbsp. heavy cream, divided

1 Tbsp. pure vanilla extract

1 cup creamy peanut butter

1¾ cups powdered sugar

1 cup semisweet chocolate chips

3 Tbsp. corn syrup

DIRECTIONS

Line an 8-inch square cake pan with parchment paper with a 2-inch overhang of paper on all sides.

Melt 4 Tbsp. butter in a medium saucepan over medium-high heat. Add the brown sugar, ½ cup cream and the vanilla. Bring to a boil. Let boil for 2 minutes, stirring constantly. Add the peanut butter and stir until smooth. Take off the heat and let cool for 5 minutes.

Put the peanut butter mixture in a mixer preferably fitted with a paddle attachment. Mix on medium-low speed and gradually add the powdered sugar. Mix until everything is incorporated and smooth. Put the mixture in the prepared pan and smooth the top with a spatula.

In a small saucepan, melt the remaining 1 Tbsp. butter with the chocolate chips and corn syrup. Add the remaining 3 Tbsp. of cream and mix until smooth. Pour over the top of the peanut butter fudge and refrigerate until firm, at least 2 hours.

Cut into small squares and serve.

WAYNE FAMILY TIP

To guarantee your fudge has the perfect consistency, use a thermometer to make sure you are cooking it between 237 to 239 degrees F.

VANILLA WAFER COCONUT CAKE

If you're on the hunt for an easy to-make, hard-to-turn-down dessert, your quest is now at an end.

SERVES 10

SUPPLIES

- 1 stick butter, at room temperature, plus more for preparing the pan
- Flour, for preparing the pan
- 1½ cups sugar
- 1 tsp. pure vanilla extract
- 6 large eggs
- 2 (6.3-oz.) boxes vanilla wafers, very finely crushed
- ½ cup coconut milk
- 1 (7-oz.) bag coconut flakes
- 1 cup chopped pecans

DIRECTIONS

Grease and flour a bundt cake pan very well. Preheat oven to 300 degrees F.

Cream the butter and sugar together in a mixer for 3 minutes. Add the vanilla and beat in. Add the eggs, one at a time, beating well and scraping down the sides after each addition.

Stir in half the crushed cookies, then the coconut milk, then the remaining half of the cookies. Mix well. Save a handful of the coconut for garnish and stir the rest into the batter along with the pecans. Pour the batter into the prepared cake pan and bake for 1 hour 30 minutes.

Let the cake cool in the pan. Flip onto a serving plate and garnish with coconut flakes.

WAYNE FAMILY TIP

For additional garnish, drizzle caramel sauce over the cake. It pairs perfectly with the vanilla goodness you've whipped together.

Duke and son Patrick play chess on the set of *McLintock!* (1963). John Wayne was a huge fan of the game and played every chance he could get.

PATRIOTIC PAVLOVA

This bountiful, berry and cream-filled meringue dessert tastes as good as it looks. And that's saying something.

SERVES 6

SUPPLIES

- 4 large egg whites, room temperature
- Pinch of kosher or sea salt
- 1 cup sugar
- 2 tsp. cornstarch
- 1 tsp. white vinegar
- 1 tsp. vanilla extract
- 1 cup cold heavy whipping cream
- 1 Tbsp. powdered sugar
- 1 (12-oz.) package fresh or frozen raspberries (thawed if frozen)
- 1 tsp. balsamic vinegar (optional)
- ½ pint fresh raspberries
- 1 pint fresh blueberries

DIRECTIONS

Preheat oven to 180 degrees F.

Draw a 9-inch circle on one side of a piece of parchment paper using a cake or pie pan as a guide. Flip the parchment over so the circle is on the reverse side and place on a sheet pan.

Beat egg whites with salt in a large mixing bowl until they start to firm up, about 1 minute. With the mixer going slowly, add the sugar and continue to beat until it forms firm, shiny peaks, about 2 minutes.

Sift the cornstarch onto the egg whites and add the vinegar and vanilla. Fold lightly with a spatula. Pile the egg white mixture onto the parchment paper in the center of the circle and gently smooth the mixture to fill the circle starting from the middle and working out in all directions until you have a round disk.

Bake for 1 hour 30 minutes and then turn off the oven and let cool completely in the oven.

Beat heavy whipping cream with powdered sugar until it forms soft peaks. Do not over beat.

Put thawed frozen raspberries and balsamic vinegar (if using) in a blender and blend until smooth. Strain through a sieve if you do not like the seeds.

When the pavlova is completely cooled, peel off the parchment paper and place on plate or serving platter. Spread whipped cream evenly over the pavlova leaving about ½ inch border of meringue then ring the whipped cream with the raspberries and fill the center with the blueberries.

Spoon the raspberry sauce over and serve.

WAYNE FAMILY TIP

This dessert is best eaten the day of, so have your guests come hungry.

Duke takes in a ballgame with son Michael (far left), brother Robert (far right) and a friend. John Wayne would help introduce a new generation of Americans to the game by sponsoring Little League teams.

CRANBERRY PIE

When the family is clamoring for a tart treat, turn to this recipe to keep them happy.

SERVES 8

SUPPLIES

Pie

1 package piecrust mix

12 Tbsp. cold butter, cut into small pieces

8 Tbsp. cold vegetable shortening

6-8 Tbsp. ice cold water

1 (12-oz.) bag fresh cranberries (3 cups)

5 ripe pears, peeled, seeded and cut into 1-inch chunks

¾ cup pure maple syrup

1 Tbsp. pure vanilla extract

6 Tbsp. cornstarch

½ tsp. kosher salt

1 egg yolk

1 Tbsp. heavy cream

1 Tbsp. turbinado sugar (or other coarse sugar)

Whipped Cream

1 cup heavy cream

2 Tbsp. pure maple syrup

1 tsp. pure vanilla extract

DIRECTIONS

Prepare the pie crust according to the directions on the bag using the butter, shortening and water. Divide into 2 disks, wrap in plastic wrap and refrigerate for 1 hour.

Place a piece of waxed or parchment paper on a work surface, top with one of the disks of dough then another piece of paper and roll into a circle a little larger than a 9-inch pie plate. Remove the top sheet of paper, place the pie plate on top of the dough and flip the dough and plate over. Remove the paper and gently fit the dough into the pie plate.

In a large bowl, combine the cranberries, pear chunks, ¾ cup maple syrup, vanilla, cornstarch and salt. Pour the filling into the pie crust and gently press down to make the filling as even as possible.

Roll out the second disk between the two sheets of waxed or parchment paper and cut it with a 1 to 1 ½ inch cookie cutter. Place the cutouts on the pie, overlapping slightly until the whole top is covered with some spaces between the cutouts. Refrigerate the pie while the oven is preheating.

Wrap a large baking sheet with foil and place on the bottom rack of the oven (to catch any spills from the pie and keep your oven clean). Position the other rack in the center and preheat the oven to 375 degrees F.

Once the oven has preheated, remove the pie from the refrigerator. Mix the egg yolk and cream together and brush generously over the

WAYNE FAMILY TIP

To avoid having a soggy pie, sprinkle your pie crust with a little bit of flour before adding the filling.

cutouts on top of the pie. Sprinkle with the turbinado sugar. Bake pie on the center rack of the oven for 90 minutes. After about 50 minutes of baking, place a piece of foil on top of the pie to keep the crust from becoming too brown. Let pie cool before serving.

Whipped Cream

Combine the cream, maple syrup and vanilla and beat until soft peaks form. Serve a dollop of the sweetened cream on top of each slice of pie.

OVER-THE-TOP CHOCOLATE CAKE

A rich and decadent dessert that you might want to save for a special occasion. Or, you know, the weekend.

SERVES 12

SUPPLIES

Cake

- 3 cups all-purpose flour, plus more for the pans
- ⅔ cup unsweetened cocoa powder
- 2 tsp. instant coffee or espresso powder
- 2 tsp. baking soda
- 1 tsp. kosher salt
- 2 cups sugar
- 2 cups unsweetened rice milk or coconut milk
- 1 cup mayonnaise
- 1 Tbsp. vanilla extract
- 3 Tbsp. agave nectar

Frosting

- 1¼ cups plus 2 Tbsp. unsweetened cocoa powder
- 3 cups vegetable shortening
- 1½ cups maple syrup
- 1 Tbsp. vanilla extract
- 2 tsp. instant coffee or espresso powder
- ¼ tsp. kosher salt

DIRECTIONS

Make the cake: Preheat the oven to 350 degrees F. Spray two 9-inch cake pans with cooking spray. Add some flour to the pans. Tilt and rotate the pans to coat with flour, tapping out any excess. Cut pieces of parchment paper to fit in the bottom of the pans. Place in the pans and spray the paper lightly with more cooking spray.

In a large mixing bowl, whisk together the flour, cocoa powder, coffee or espresso powder, baking soda and salt. In another mixing bowl, whisk together the sugar, milk, mayonnaise, vanilla extract and agave. Add the wet ingredients to the dry and stir until fully combined. Divide the batter evenly between the prepared pans and bake for 30 minutes or until a toothpick inserted in the center comes out clean. Let cool in the pans for 10 minutes, then remove to a wire rack to finish cooling.

Make the frosting: Put the cocoa powder in the bowl of an electric mixer fitted with the paddle attachment. Turn the mixer on low and mix until the cocoa powder is free of lumps. Add the remaining frosting ingredients and, starting on low speed, mix the ingredients, gradually increasing the speed to high and mixing until all ingredients are well combined. Once combined, scrape down the sides and bottom of the mixing bowl with a rubber spatula, then beat on high speed until the frosting is light and fluffy. Refrigerate the frosting to firm up.

WAYNE FAMILY TIP

Make sure to preheat your oven to minimize the time the cake batter sits at room temperature. The longer batter sits on the counter, the greater chance it won't rise properly.

Cut a strip of waxed paper and place it on a cake platter to keep your platter clean while frosting. Using a sharp knife or piece of unflavored dental floss, cut the cakes in half horizontally. Place one half of one cake, top side down, on the waxed paper. Spread some frosting on top of the cake and top with the other half of the cake, cut side down. Spread some frosting on top of that layer, then place the bottom half of the other cake, bottom side down, on top. Frost the layer and top with the last cake half, cut side down. Frost the sides and top of the cake. Remove the piece of waxed paper. Refrigerate the cake until 5 to 10 minutes before serving.

Duke and his wife Pilar with daughter Aissa and newborn son Ethan. The Wayne family moved to Newport Beach, California, right aroud the time of Ethan's birth.

Duke in a scene from *The Longest Day* (1962). The World War II epic cost $10 million to make, a staggering figure by the budgets of the day.

Conversion Guide

Use this handy chart to convert cups and ounces to liters and grams.

//

Volume

¼ teaspoon = 1 mL

½ teaspoon = 2 mL

1 teaspoon = 5 mL

1 tablespoon = 15 mL

¼ cup = 50 mL

⅓ cup = 75 mL

½ cup = 125 mL

⅔ cup = 150 mL

¾ cup = 175 mL

1 cup = 250 mL

1 quart = 1 liter

1½ quarts = 1.5 liters

2 quarts = 2 liters

2½ quarts = 2.5 liters

3 quarts = 3 liters

4 quarts = 4 liters

Weight

1 ounce = 30 grams

2 ounces = 55 grams

3 ounces = 85 grams

4 ounces (¼ pound) = 115 grams

8 ounces (½ pound) = 225 grams

16 ounces (1 pound) = 455 grams

1 pound = 455 grams

2 pounds = 910 grams

Length

⅛ inch = 3 mm

¼ inch = 6 mm

½ inch = 13 mm

¾ inch = 19 mm

1 inch = 2.5 cm

2 inches = 5 cm

Temperatures

Fahrenheit	Celsius
32°	**0°**
212°	100°
250°	120°
275°	140°
300°	150°
325°	160°
350°	180°
375°	190°
400°	200°
425°	220°
450°	230°
475°	240°
500°	260°

INDEX

Duke and family are ready to set sail. John Wayne loved taking his loved ones out on the water, and favorite destinations included Catalina Island.

Media Lab Books
For inquiries, call 646-838-6637

Copyright 2016 Topix Media Lab

Published by Topix Media Lab
14 Wall Street, Suite 4B
New York, NY 10005

Printed in China

ISBN-10: 1-942556-30-6
ISBN-13: 978-1-942556-30-5

Photos and recipes adapted from Carol Kicinski and Stephanie O'Dea. All other photos used with permission of John Wayne Enterprises except:
Andrew Cebulka/Stocksy: Cover. AF Archive/Alamy: p110, 189. Globe Photos/ImageCollect: p5, 154, 250. Pictorial Press Ltd/Alamy: p124, 176. Photos
12/Alamy: p16, 69. Trinity Mirror/Mirrorpix/Alamy: p210. ZUMAPress/Alamy: p148. iStock: p54. Shutterstock: p217.Abramson/ImageCollect: Back Cover.

The mission of the John Wayne Cancer Foundation is to bring courage, strength and grit to the fight against cancer. *www.johnwayne.org*